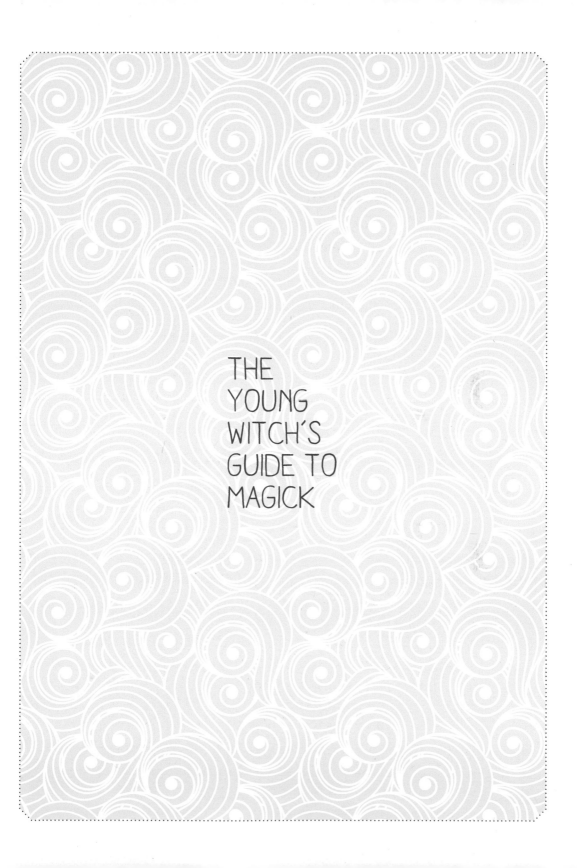

THE
YOUNG
WITCH'S
GUIDE TO
MAGICK

THE YOUNG WITCH'S GUIDE TO MAGICK

CASSANDRA EASON

STERLING CHILDREN'S BOOKS
New York

STERLING CHILDREN'S BOOKS
New York

An Imprint of Sterling Publishing Co., Inc.
1166 Avenue of the Americas
New York, NY 10036

ISBN 978-1-4549-3685-5

Distributed in Canada by Sterling Publishing Co., Inc.
c/o Canadian Manda Group, 664 Annette Street
Toronto, Ontario M6S 2C8, Canada
Distributed in the United Kingdom by GMC Distribution Services
Castle Place, 166 High Street, Lewes, East Sussex BN7 1XU, England
Distributed in Australia by NewSouth Books
University of New South Wales, Sydney, NSW 2052, Australia

For information about custom editions, special sales, and premium and corporate purchases,
please contact Sterling Special Sales at 800-805-5489 or specialsales@sterlingpublishing.com.

Manufactured in South Korea

Lot #:
2 4 6 8 10 9 7 5 3 1
05/20

sterlingpublishing.com

Cover and interior design by Irene Vandervoort
Cover and interior illustrations by Laura Tolton

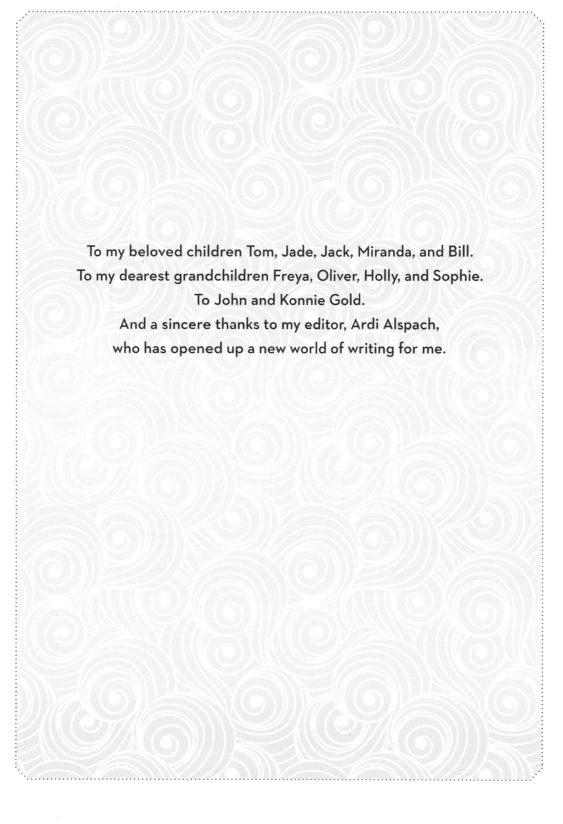

To my beloved children Tom, Jade, Jack, Miranda, and Bill.
To my dearest grandchildren Freya, Oliver, Holly, and Sophie.
To John and Konnie Gold.
And a sincere thanks to my editor, Ardi Alspach,
who has opened up a new world of writing for me.

CONTENTS

✴ YOUR JOURNEY TO MAGICK ✴

So, apprentice witches, welcome to witch school! I will be sharing with you magick secrets I have learned over many years. Before long, you and your friends will be sending magick through the cosmos, whether you cast your spells alone in your special magickal place or have magickal candlelit evenings with friends when the moon is shining bright.

Magick can make your everyday world better by sending out *notice me* vibes to that special guy or girl or *don't mess with me* messages to bullies waiting in the schoolyard or *let's be fair* signals to the roommate with attitude who lays claim to the best bed in the college dorm.

We all have the power to make good things happen and get rid of what makes life bad.

This book will teach you how to make your own spells, anytime, anyplace, always for good reasons, and for absolutely any wish using whatever is around the home, garden, or wherever you hang out. You can use materials like flower petals, your favorite jewelry, candles, balloons, bubbles, ribbons, scarves, sewing thread, clay, and other art supplies as you craft your own magickal space and rituals. You will also learn how to do spells to protect yourself against online bullying, jealousy, and family problems.

You should never do harm in magick, but it's not always practical to say to someone before doing magick, "Hey, do you mind if I do a spell to stop you from making put-down remarks about my appearance when we are with people we don't know?"

For a start, they wouldn't say yes. If you do want to stay friends, a bit of good magick input to make them kinder as you give out *respect me* vibes does no harm. Of course you can't and shouldn't force people to do things against their will, but sending out loving vibes is good. And if the spell's purpose isn't right at the time, it will open you to better purposes.

So, let's try a spell. You only need some salt and a white candle for this spell. In **CHAPTER 1** we'll talk about tools and other items to help you set up that beautiful magickal place—or altar, as we witches call it—in your bedroom, but for now, we'll keep it simple.

FOR WHATEVER YOU MOST WANT OR NEED IN THE WORLD

* Light a white candle.

* Sprinkle a pinch of salt into the flame so it sparkles.

* Say what it is you wish for nine times, faster and faster.

* After the ninth time, clap your hands in front of the candle and quickly blow out the candle, saying, *"Wish be mine as I count nine, eight, seven, six, five, four, three, two, one. The spell is done! May my wish swiftly come."*

* That was easy, wasn't it? And if you can *do* anything nonmagickal to make that wish come true faster, that will help the magick happen faster, too.

CHAPTER 1

❋ YOUR MAGICKAL ALTAR ❋

Of course, you can cast spells absolutely anywhere, anytime! Maybe on the school bus, during lunch, on the dance floor to help that cute guy notice you, to give you an extra boost of confidence before a big test, or to help your bully get caught in the act. But your altar, or special magickal place, is where you will do most of your spellcasting, and the more you use it, the more magickal it will become. If you are at college, you may be able to team up with friends to create a sacred place you can all share.

Over weeks and months, it will become a special place where sometimes you just light a candle or some incense, hold your favorite crystal, or allow wishes and dreams to come and go without any special ceremony.

FOR YOUR ALTAR YOU WILL NEED:

- ❋   First, a box with a lock to keep your tools private and safe.

- ❋   You will also want a table or flat surface. You can cover it with a scarf or a cloth made of velvet or sparkly fabric, decorated with moons, suns, zodiac signs, etc.

❋ You should also have a white candle in the center. From this candle you will light all the other candles used in your spells. Because all colors are contained in white, white candles can be used for every kind of magick. Later, when you learn the magickal meanings of different colors, you can use a candle color that fits the intent of the spell.

❋ Place a small dish in the center near the white candle. This will hold the crystal, piece of jewelry, or charm that you will be filling with magickal power. You can carry this symbol of the spell with you or wear it after the magick work is done. If you want to be really witchy, buy a dish with a pentacle on it from a new age store or online, or you can paint or draw one on an ordinary dish.

The five-pointed star, or pentacle, is a very old symbol that brings together all the different parts of magick. Each point represents a magickal element: Earth, Air, Fire, Water, and Spirit.

A simple pentacle

THE FOUR QUARTERS

Traditionally, magick is cast in a circle, and the circle is divided into four quarters, each standing for a different power or element: Earth, Air, Fire, and Water. Mixed together, these elements give the power to bring magick wishes into the everyday world.

Each quarter has its own special item that represents it: salt is used for Earth, incense for Air, a candle for Fire, and a bowl of water for Water.

Each quarter also has its own magickal tool: in Earth it's a bell, in Air it's a knife called an athame, in the Fire quarter it's a wand, and in Water it's a chalice, though you won't be using these until you are doing longer magickal celebrations.

SETTING UP THE ALTAR

Think of your altar, whatever shape table you are using, as a clock face flat on the table, and imagine it divided into four quarters.

In the 12 o'clock position—the Earth Quarter—put a dish of salt, dried flower petals or fresh fragrant flower petals (you should replace these regularly), rose or lavender potpourri, or any dried herbs (the kind you buy in the supermarket should work just fine). Place a bell or Tibetan bells in this quarter as well.

At the 3 o'clock position—the Air Quarter—place two incense sticks in holders (the sort that catch the ash), facing each other. You can use scents like sandalwood, frankincense, myrrh, rose, or lavender. These are very special scents that have been used in magick for hundreds of years, but feel free to use your favorite. Also put in a silver-colored letter opener, which will work as your athame or ritual knife. Over the coming months, you will use this knife in spells more and more.

At the 6 o'clock position—the Fire Quarter—place a red, orange, or gold candle in a holder.

Also, put a magick wand in the Fire Quarter. You can buy a real wand from new age stores or online, but a smooth twig pointed at one end or a long clear quartz crystal pointed at one end and rounded at the other is just as good.

In the 9 o'clock position—the Water Quarter—place a small dish of

 TIP:

If you want to melt wax to make a charm or love image, use candles made of beeswax or any candle where the color goes all the way through.

water or a vial of your favorite fragrance. When doing special celebration spells, put a wine glass or goblet made of metal or glass, called a chalice, filled with juice here as well.

CHARGING YOUR ALTAR

Now that you have set up your altar, it is time to carry out a ceremony to make it your very own special place. We call this "dedicating the altar." Just follow the step-by-step instructions below. You will probably want to read over them a few times or create a checklist to follow during the ceremony.

Make sure you won't be disturbed by the dog, your roommate, or your parents. If you wish, invite a special friend along to share the magick.

1. If your altar is against the wall, pull it out so you can walk all the way around it.

2. Play soft music and light your central candle, the red/gold candle in the Fire Quarter, and the incense sticks, saying, *"May my magick always be beautiful."*

3. Ring the bell clockwise around that altar, beginning at the Earth Quarter, and then in the center of the altar.

4. Put the salt and water bowls side by side in the middle of the altar, then drop nine pinches of salt into the water bowl.

5. Stir the water with the athame clockwise. Then, as you walk around the altar table clockwise, starting at the Earth Quarter, sprinkle water all around on the ground, saying, *"May my magick always be beautiful"* again.

6. Put the bowls back in their quarters.

7. Take one of your lighted incense sticks in each hand, and walk around the altar clockwise, again starting at the Earth Quater, making smoke spirals, saying, *"I promise only to do magick for the greatest good."* Put the incense back in its place.

8. Pick up your wand with the pointed end outward and walk again clockwise around your altar, touching each of the items, starting with the salt bowl, and saying, *"May only light and loveliness enter here in this, my magickal place."*

9. Return the wand to its place.

10. Ring the bell all around and in the center of the altar, moving counterclockwise, then blow out the candle and leave the incense to burn.

11. Empty the water bowl and put it back in its place on the altar.

12. Finally, hold your hands with your palms outward toward your altar and say, *"This is my private place and space. Magickal guardians keep it safe."*

13. Do this once a week to keep your altar fresh and magickal.

CHAPTER 2
✳ YOUR MAGICKAL ✳ TREASURE BOX

You will often want to cast a spell in a hurry, and nothing is more annoying than finding you've run out of yellow candles if you're trying out for a spot on a sports team the next morning. Over time, you will build up a collection of magickal items you can store in a special treasure box that lives under your altar. This can be as beautifully decorated or as plain as you wish! You can often pick up a magick treasure box about the size of a small suitcase at a yard sale, or an older relative may have an old-fashioned cabin trunk you can use, the kind that looks like a pirate's treasure chest. It's also a good idea to keep a checklist of items you want to keep in stock inside your treasure box at all times. I've included a list of suggested items below.

WHAT TO KEEP IN YOUR MAGICKAL TREASURE BOX

Witches become a bit like magpies or squirrels, collecting things like beautiful pieces of ribbon, broken beads, loose pearls, and glass nuggets in different colors (the kind people put in flower vases are ideal if you don't have the right crystal for a spell in color magick). After all, what don't you collect?

You should keep regular candles in different colors handy as well as beeswax candles for melting to make figures (to represent family, love, and healing) or for writing magickal messages in the cooling melted wax to keep as charms. I have listed the color meanings in **CHAPTER 5**.

Incense sticks in different fragrances are good to keep on hand as well. You can choose powerful ones like frankincense or basil for success and money if your allowance is getting low, sage and rosemary for exams and study, and rose or lavender for love or good luck. (See **CHAPTER 7** to learn about the magickal meanings of flowers.)

Keep one or two fragrance oils in your treasure box for mixing into spell bags. Again, frankincense is a must for a lot of oomph, myrrh is wonderful for gentler spells, and lemongrass is good for protection against harmful people.

You should always have sewing thread as well as ribbons in different colors and lengths for tying magickal knots.

Add in a few jars of dried cooking herbs, such as basil, rosemary, and sage to mix into herbal spell bags and, if you can get them, dried lavender, chamomile flowers, and rose petals.

> ✳ TIP:
>
> You can open herbal tea bags for chamomile flowers or hard-to-get herbs. Herbal tea bags made into teas and strained are good for sprinkling around a spell item instead of water or enchanting in a spell to make a magickal tea.

Potpourri can be made magickal in a spell and put in bowls around the home if there are a lot of quarrels. You can also use it instead of salt for the Earth power in a spell.

Rose water (obtainable from a pharmacy or you can make your own) is important to have, as you can sprinkle it around your room if it feels spooky, put on your inner wrists to make you feel beautiful if you've got a zit, or use it in a spell instead of water. Matches are also helpful because you never know when you will want to light a candle to make a wish. Extra dishes are useful for holding enchanted herbs or flower petals to keep the magick flowing around your room.

For the metals used in magick spellwork, you can use coins of any value (silver, gold-colored, or copper).

Modeling clay in different colors is ideal for making figures for protection or friendship, to call love, or for fixing family problems.

Collect symbols for spells, such as small models (raid children's toy boxes), or go to garage sales for old charm bracelets for charms of boats, planes, and cars for travel, or a silver horseshoe for good luck. Tiny fabric dolls like worry dolls are also great as representations of family members or friends, with one for yourself in the center of the others, if, for example, you want to be more popular or someone is shutting you out of the friendship group.

Paper and pens in different colors can be used for writing wishes.

You will also want to include crystals of different kinds and colors. You will learn more about these in **CHAPTER 6**. You need only buy or collect small ones.

MAKING YOUR MAGICKAL SPELL BOOK

Start a special book with a velvet or beautifully patterned cover, called in magick your "Book of Shadows." This is something you only share with your closest friends who are witches, too. Have a section to remind you what the different colors mean and add information on magickal herbs, crystals, and moon phases as you work through the book so you have a quick reminder of all the information you need for magick at hand.

Copy into your Book of Shadows any special spells you create or that I have suggested at the end of chapters. You can make notes on your computer and use your book to copy those spells you want to keep. It's also useful to have a working notebook so you can jot things down when you are out and about, or keep a section on your tablet or smartphone for quick notes with dates, especially if you have accessed an online moon calendar.

CHAPTER 3
✳ SPELLCASTING 101 ✳

Though this book is filled with spells ready for you to cast, you will want to create and cast your own spells so they are exactly what you want, how you want, and when you want.

Spells have a step-by-step structure, making them easy to create and follow, the same way you follow the same steps every time for most processes. For example, when you download a movie onto your tablet or computer, you follow a certain procedure. After downloading the first time, that procedure became automatic. It is the same with magick.

You already have your altar set up with tools and symbols, so now we are going to use them to cast spells. Sometimes, as with my instant spells, the stages flow into one another. Once you know how spellcasting works, it doesn't matter how fast or slow you cast—it becomes second nature.

Read through this chapter before creating and casting your first spell, and perhaps the first couple of times you can get a friend to read the instructions aloud as you follow them. If you prefer doing spellwork by yourself, record yourself reading the steps out loud.

CHOOSING YOUR WITCH NAME

Every witch has a secret name he or she uses when casting magick spells. You should tell no one except close magickal friends. If you are working as a magickal group, often called a coven (more on that later), you can tell them, too. Once you have your special witch name, you can start a spell as you light your central candle by saying, "I am (say your secret name), and I am casting this spell. . . ." You might choose as your secret witch name the name of a crystal you love, a flower, a tree, a goddess or god, or a magickal hero/ine from a series you watch on TV. I know a lot of "Galadriel" witches named after the Elven queen in *Lord of the Rings*.

You can also write your magickal name in incense stick smoke or using the index finger of your active hand (the hand you write with) over your special possessions, like your smartphone, memory stick, ring, or pendant, to fill them with your own power and to magickally attach them to you. In this way, you won't lose them or have them stolen, and you can also, by adding a wish, fill whatever is yours with the powers you most need at anytime, bound by your magickal name.

Write your magickal name in incense smoke over your altar and private possessions to keep out curious or interfering family members and friends.

PSYCHIC PROTECTION

As long as you never cast spells with bad intentions, your guardian angels or spirit guides will keep you safe. A lot of witches work with angels, whether they are Christians or not, because angels are a good way to visualize the protection of good higher beings. It is your choice how you picture these guardians.

Here is a very special archangel protection spell witches through the ages have found very reassuring when they want to keep out any mischievous spirits or when they need to banish their own angry feelings or fears. You may substitute your own kind of spirit guide in this spell if you wish.

THE FOUR ARCHANGELS OF PROTECTION

To begin, put a couple of drops of fragrance into a shallow dish. Rose or lavender are very protective, but if you use one you really like, that will have your own power already in it. Dip the index finger of your writing hand into the fragrance and put a drop in the center of your hairline, the center of your brow, the base of your throat, and your two inner wrist points. (These are special invisible power centers within your body, often called chakras, and by protecting them with fragrance you protect your body and mind from any harm.) Then say, "Guardians of light (or angels) protect me as I cast my spells."

There are four special archangels we can call on to stand around us and keep us safe as we work with magick.

Uriel is called Guardian of the Earth and Sun who brought magick with metals to humankind. He is Archangel of Protection and holds a fiery sword.

Raphael is Archangel of Healing and the four winds. He carries a golden flask of medicine with his traveler's staff, wearing sparkling yellow robes, the colors of early morning sunlight.

Michael is Archangel of the Sun, with his gleaming gold sword and shield. He is the supreme archangel who oversees the natural world and the weather. He is also leader of all the great warrior angels and traditional dragon slayer.

Finally, there is starry and silvery Gabriel, Archangel of the

Moon, who carries divine messages and is often considered female. She has a crescent moon for her halo, a golden horn and white lily or a lantern in her right hand, and a mirror made of jasper in her left.

Before you begin your spell, call on Archangel Uriel to stand in front of you and enfold you in his wings. Then ask Raphael to stand on your right side, keeping you safe from all harm.

Next ask Michael to stand behind you with his gold shield guarding you, and finally ask Gabriel to be on your left hand to take away all fear.

The Archangel Blessing

If you wish, you can say the following words aloud or in your mind before casting a spell. If alone, turn in a clockwise circle, saying, "Before me, Uriel stands fierce and proud, Raphael to my right takes my hand, Michael uplifts me, and Gabriel takes away all fear."

Then turn again, saying, "Uriel, Raphael, Michael, and Gabriel protect me and guide me in my magickal work."

ANIMAL AND BIRD GUARDIANS

If you don't feel comfortable working with the archangels, you can call upon a power or spirit animal to stand around you. Choose one from each element to be your guardian.

Earth: the antelope, badger, bear, bull, dog, stag, or wolf

Air: the eagle, hawk, falcon, or any bird of prey

Fire: the lion/ess, cougar, fire dragon, or the legendary golden Phoenix

Water: the dolphin, whale, swan, or herons/cranes

NATURE GUARDIANS

If you love nature, perhaps you would prefer the ancient elemental fey people. These are powerful beings who ride the storms.

Ahead of you stands Geb, the Earth King elemental, whose throne is covered with crystals, silver, and gold. He is guardian of those nature spirits who live or work in the Earth or guard its treasures.

To your right stands Paralda, the mysterious winged Queen of the Sylphs, who lives on the highest mountain on earth. She rules the sylphs, who are winged air spirits that live for hundreds of years. They reside on mountain tops.

Behind you stands Djinn, a being made of pure fire, who is never still and rules all fire spirits. Or you might prefer a salamander.

To your left stands Niksa, who rises from the sea, translucent and rainbow colored, riding a giant seahorse or in a pearly or sea-green chariot pulled by white seahorses. She has long flowing hair knotted with shells and a swirling cloak in all the colors of the sea, edged with pearls.

Turn in a circle, slowly opening your arms to each of them.

CLOSING DOWN

After a spell, end by thanking your angels, animals, or nature beings, and blow out any candles you have lit. Leave incense to burn itself out. It is always important, even with angels, to wish them goodbye and say, "Until we meet again," otherwise their energies will buzz around.

Indoors or out, press your

feet hard into the ground and point your fingers downward and together to return into the earth any free-floating energies that might unsettle you.

CASTING A SPELL

Now it is time to learn to cast a spell.

Before you start the spell, go back and reread PAGES 7–9 so you are sure of the positions of the candles, incense, salt, wand, and other tools on your altar. Make sure everything is in its place. You may want to read the spellcasting steps below two or three times before casting a spell. You could also write yourself a list of the stages for the first spell or two you cast.

STAGE 1: Decide on the reason why you are casting the spell.

This can be just three or four words or, if you like, an original poem.

STAGE 2: Choose a symbol to represent your spell's goal.

You will fill the symbol with power as you work the spell, and afterward you can carry or wear it to bring good luck or to help bring into the everyday world whatever you asked for.

The following make good spell symbols:

* A crystal pendant you can wear for luck or protection after casting the spell

* A plant to be sent after a get-well spell for a sick grandmother

* Coins in a pot if you are saving for something special like your first car or an extraordinary vacation

* A written message on colored paper and ink

* A photograph of the person you want to attract or animal you want to help

* Small fabric dolls or ones made from modeling clay, dough, or melted beeswax to stand for a person

STAGE 3: Gathering the magick.

1. Put the symbol in the dish in the center of your altar.

2. Ask your four spirit guides or archangels to protect you using the protection spells on PAGES 132-134.

3. Light each candle being used in the spell, starting with the candle in the center, saying as you light each, "I (secret name) do ask for (name spell wish)."

4. Light the incense sticks from the central candle.

5. Lift the symbol dish up toward the central candle and say again what you are wishing for.

STAGE 4: Setting the spell energies in motion (see PAGE 28 to learn about the Four Quarters).

Go to the Earth Quarter on the altar.

Sprinkle three circles of salt clockwise around the symbol dish and say your wish three times. I often use a chant such as
Power of the magick, power of the spell, power of the magick, use the magick well instead of repeating the spell words, as this works well to raise the energy. You can of course create your own chant. Return the salt to its place.

Go to the Air Quarter on the altar.

Hold an incense stick in each hand like a smoke pen, draw smoke spirals clockwise around the symbol dish three times clockwise, and again say your chosen words three times. Return the incense sticks to their holder.

Go to the Fire Quarter on the altar.

Pass the symbol dish three times around the red, orange, or gold candle and say the same words three times. Return the symbol dish to the center.

Go to the Water Quarter on the altar.

Sprinkle three circles of water clockwise around the symbol dish and say the same words three times. Return the bowl to its place.

STAGE 5: Increasing the power of the spell.

Now, holding your wand in your writing hand, circle it clockwise faster and faster while facing the altar and saying the words you previously used. Say them faster and faster.

Continue moving the wand and speaking even faster until you feel that the power of the spell has reached its height.

STAGE 6: Releasing the power.

When you feel the moment is right, release the power into the cosmos by lifting your wand in the air and then bringing it down fast by your side and up again, ending with it touching the symbol.

Say, "The Power is free, the wish is mine, the power's in me, wish fly free" (or words that feel right to you to let the power free).

STAGE 7: Ending the Spell.

Hold the symbol, blow out the candles, and thank your guardians. Press down with your feet hard, fingers pointing downward, to bring yourself back to the everyday world, and then tidy your altar.

Keep the symbol somewhere close to you, like in a bedside drawer or, if jewelry, wear it so you can feel the power of the spell in the days ahead.

CHAPTER 4

✳ CIRCLE CASTING ✳

Like all modern witches, a lot of your best spells will be cast on the move and, in many instances, after asking for the protection of spirits. But when you want to do a special spell, you can use your altar or make an outdoor altar with a flat rock or picnic table.

The circle is one of the oldest and most magickal ways of putting protection around ourselves while we are casting spells. It creates a magickal enclosed space in which the power of the spell grows as the different ingredients of the spell mix. Because you are working with magickal powers, your circle also prevents any unfriendly spirits or mischievous nature beings from interfering.

INSTANT CIRCLE CASTING

For a spell in a hurry, you can cast an instant circle around your altar or magickal working space. Start by pointing straight ahead at waist height with your writing hand, palm facing down, fingers together, and thumb tucked in. Turn in a clockwise circle while standing on the same spot, beginning at the Earth Quarter. From your fingers, imagine blue or gold light spreading all around you and your altar, like shimmering star walls rising so you and your spell area are covered in light.

Some people picture this as standing in a beautiful temple open to the stars. Imagine your magick wishes, set free in the spell, rising like a cone of rainbow laser beams that break into stars like a firework display. If you are on the school bus, you can create in your mind a beautiful bubble of light around yourself or a rainbow web. Keep practicing your visualization until you can call powerful energies around you when you need to.

CASTING YOUR CIRCLES

There are different ways of casting magickal circles. You can have a circle as your phone background, such as a photo of an ancient stone circle. You can create an invisible one by tracing with your fingers on the surface of your desk or workspace, imagining the light enclosing you as well as the working area. This is excellent for when you feel anxious or for when you are being hassled. Maybe visualize a lioness or dragon to guard the entrance of your circle.

MAGICKAL CIRCLE CASTING

Circle casting is really easy. After you've read through this chapter, choose the type of circle you want to cast and read through it carefully before starting. If you prefer, ask a friend to guide you through it the first time. It's your choice, and before long, your favorite method of circle casting will be second nature.

If you are doing spellwork at your altar, you should light the altar candle and incense before making the circle.

Whatever the form or size of circle, start and end in the Earth Quarter.

If you are doing spellwork outside, you can draw a clockwise circle in dirt, snow, or sand with a long stick or your magick wand. Rub it out counterclockwise after the spell, or leave the circle for the weather to take

away. Chalk on paving stones works well also. For special occasions, you can use flower petals, dried herbs, or potpourri outdoors and leave it to blow away.

Make any circle sufficiently large to give you and any friends who are joining you plenty of space to move and dance. Set up or move your altar inside the circle, placing it in the center. If you are working in your bedroom, you may want to push any other furniture back against the walls so you don't bump into anything.

One special way to add some sparkle to your circle is to use tealights to outline the perimeter. Use heatproof holders or plates for each candle. The tealights do not have to be close together. Be careful not to burn yourself as you light them. You can also use battery-operated tealights if you can't have candles in your bedroom. Place them in a circle shape in advance, and moving clockwise, light each one as you call the guardians. Afterward, blow them out counterclockwise.

If you are working with a group, each person can have their own tealight and carry it lighted into the circle.

When you start a coven (see **CHAPTER 13**), it's especially magickal to make the circle out of people linking hands one by one, starting in the

Earth Quarter. As each person moves to make a circle, select one person to stand in the center to carry out the spell. He or she should turn slowly, saying softly, "The circle of love has no beginning and no end. Welcome to the circle of love."

You can also make a less visible but equally powerful circle by spiraling smoke from an incense stick held in your writing hand as you walk in a clockwise circle around your altar and spell area. You can also make a circle of water drops from your altar water bowl—into which three pinches of salt have been stirred with your athame, first clockwise and then counterclockwise, followed by a cross made on the surface of the water. Make the salt water using your altar bowls of salt and water before casting the circle.

CIRCLES OF LIGHT

This is the most used kind of magick circle, made of pictured light drawn invisibly in the air to mark out the area of your magick circle around your altar and spell area. The circle of light is enough on its own. You can, if you prefer, stand in the center with hands facing outward. Picture the light flowing from your fingers to make the circle.

Use a long pointed clear crystal, magick wand, or athame to draw your invisible light circle at about waist height.

Starting in the Earth Quarter, walk around the outside of your pictured light circle clockwise as you create it. Picture the circle as gold, white, silver, or blue light rising from the ground to make shimmering temple walls.

As you walk, say continuously, "May the circle that is cast remain unbroken, may the love I/we create remain forever in my/our heart/s, merry meet until I/we from this place depart." Step into the circle.

Finish by facing the altar and saying, "May the angels/Goddess bless this ritual."

WELCOMING THE GUARDIANS OF THE CIRCLE

Once you start casting circles and working with the four quarters of the circle, you are changing from spells to rituals. This is like dressing up for a formal dance instead of chilling out in your jeans, but of course you are still yourself and magick is still magick. As you learned in **CHAPTER 1**, imagine your circle divided into four quadrants, like our clock face on the altar, but the clock face is now on the ground.

When you do ritual magick you will use your altar tools—the bell, knife (athame pronounced ATH-uh-may), wand, and the chalice that you can fill with water or juice—a lot more. Check **PAGES 6-8** to make sure they are all in the right places on your altar.

Each quarter of the circle also has its own spiritual guardian who stands guard. They keep you safe while you are doing magick in the circle, and they are what you welcome if you are doing a longer ritual, not a day-to-day spell.

You have lots of choices for who to welcome as guardians. Some people—in magick we call them practitioners—use animals: the wolf or bear for the Earth Quarter at 12 o'clock, the eagle for the Air Quarter at 3 o'clock, the lioness or dragon for the Fire Quarter at 6 o'clock, and the owl or dolphin for the Water Quarter at 9 o'clock. These are creatures that you can imagine will keep you safe.

Or, if you prefer, you can call our old friends the archangels: Uriel the mighty protector with his torch of fire for Earth; Raphael, the healer and traveler archangel, in his yellow robes for Air; Michael, Archangel of the Sun, for Fire with his golden sword and shield; and Gabriel, the starry Archangel of the Moon for Water.

Or how about the old gods and goddesses as guardians? Imagine Flora, the Roman goddess of flowers; Horus, the young Egyptian god of the sky; Apollo, the fabulous Greek sun god; and the beautiful Aphrodite, Greek love goddess born from water. You could also picture nature spirits: the gnomes with their big boots and fabulous jewels they have dug from the earth, the graceful swanlike sylphs of the Air, the always dancing and moving fire fairies, and the lovely mermaids diving out of the waters.

Try different guardians and see which feel right for you—you might change guardians if you work in a group.

THE GREETING

After casting the circle for a ritual or longer spell, face or go to the center of the Earth Quarter. Greet the Earth Guardian you have chosen. Raise your arms high and say, "You are welcome (name your Guardian, such as Wise Mother Earth). I ask for your protection and wisdom for my/our ritual."

Do the same for the other three directions.

If you are working with a group or coven, everyone else in the circle should face the same direction, raise arms, and after you have spoken say the same words as a chorus.

Then carry out your spell/ritual as normal, adding the salt, incense, etc., as described in **CHAPTER 3**.

CLOSING DOWN THE MAGICK

When the power is released, return the symbol to the altar. This time face the Water Quarter and say, "I/we thank you for your protection. Until we meet again." Then do this at Fire, Air, and finally the Earth Quarter so you end up where you started in your guardian greetings. It is always important, even with angels, goddesses, and so on, to close everything down, or you will be buzzing all night with crazy sylphs dive-bombing your dreams.

Everyone present should do the same, raising their arms at the same time as you do, but repeating your words after you speak.

Now blow out all the candles except the central one. Uncast the circle by walking around in the opposite direction you cast it, starting at Earth and moving counterclockwise. Use your ritual knife, wand, or crystal as before, and say, "May the circle be uncast."

Draw the light back into your crystal, athame, or wand, or picture the radiance sinking into the ground as you walk.

Blow out the central candle, and say, "The ritual/ceremony is ended, blessed be."

If you built your circle with tealights, blow out any still alight in the reverse order from lighting them. If in a coven or personal group, the individuals who lit them can do this one by one.

If a natural substance like herbs or flowers formed the circle, leave them to blow away after uncasting the circle. You don't need to uncast a salt, water, or incense circle because they are absorbed by the power of your spell or ritual.

Dismantle your circle counterclockwise and put your tools in your box for next time. If you are with others, enjoy a meal and some music.

CHAPTER 5

✳ THE COLORS OF MAGICK ✳

People sometimes say, "She was green with envy when my dad bought me a car for my birthday," or, "I saw red when my boyfriend/girlfriend dumped me for my best friend."

So, witches in training, colors can be a pretty powerful way of zinging energies precisely where and how we want them to go, and you'll know most of the magickal color meanings already because we use them every day.

MAGICKAL COLORS

The easiest and best way to add color to spells is by using candles, because when you light a candle, you set free all the powers of its color.

You can also use different-colored ribbons, threads, crystals, feathers (instead of incense), flowers, colored pens and paper, or modeling clay. Outdoors, you can fly colored balloons or attach different-colored paper messages or ribbons to a kite string and set the spell flying. Wear the color to attract what you most want. You can use more than one color in a spell: for example, a pink candle for romance and a green one for the romance to last, plus red if you want to spice things up.

The Most Common Colors and What They Mean

White to call to you whatever you most want, known as attracting magick

• applying for the school you really want • starting at a new school • making wishes • if someone is sick •

Red for overcoming problems and for courage

• making someone like you a lot • trying new things • keeping you safe against angry people, bullying, and unkindness • online trolls and physical attack • dealing with selfish brothers and sisters • winning in any sport or physical activity •

Orange for happiness and for confidence

• independence, especially if your parents treat you as if you are five • dealing with teachers and lecturers who make you feel dumb • making new friends or getting invited to parties • hanging out with people you really like • moving out of home to your first place •

Yellow for studying and for protection against jealousy, spite, and lies

• to guard against people who get you into trouble and cliques who shut you out • for holidays, especially with friends without family and the best summer camp ever • adventure trips and extreme sports • homework if you hate it • when you need to be early or on time and hate getting out of bed • studying and learning new things • understanding and getting the latest technology •

Green for good luck and for loyalty in love and friendships

• changing bad luck • for twin-soul love • feeling and looking attractive • becoming more popular • dealing with envious classmates • dealing with students who steal your ideas and people who try to break up your friendships • happiness with your family • overcoming overprotective parents •

Blue for success in examinations, driving tests, interviews, and internships

• getting voted leader or president of the year or captain of the sports team • overseas or interstate travel or backpacking • overcoming unfairness and prejudice at school • dealing with rivals who use dirty tricks against you •

Purple for developing your psychic powers and for protection against scary ghosts

• developing your writing and artistic gifts • for writing the best profile ever to sell yourself • overcoming fears, bad habits, and phobias • ending love relationships and friendships gone wrong without conflict •

Pink for mending quarrels and for first love and romance

• learning to trust again after someone has let you down • happiness at home • liking yourself the way you look right now even if you get teased for being different • caring for kids, whether babysitting or working at summer camp •

Brown for getting money when you are broke and for feeling safe

• for special pets • finding the right vacation or weekend job or getting an allowance increase • for good relations with older family members • feeling safe if your family, love, school life, or community is chaotic or dangerous • fun outdoors •

Silver for all kinds of magick and for beautiful dreams

• moon magick • learning witchcraft • magick under the stars
or by the ocean or river • moving into harmony with your body,
especially if you have food or image issues • keeping or
finding out secrets •

Gold for big dreams and ambitions

• fame and fortune through your talents • aiming high and
achieving it • magick when it is sunny • appearing on reality TV,
modeling, or becoming a celebrity in your teens • being asked
to join the in-crowd at school or college •

CHAPTER 6

* MAGICKAL CRYSTALS, *
GEMS, AND METALS

Gems and crystals are millions of years old and are therefore very powerful. Any symbols drawn on them will absorb their ancient power. What is more, because each crystal, metal, and gem has a magickal meaning in itself as well as the power of its color, any magick you do with them is doubled. Magick just gets better and better the more you add to a spell.

CHOOSING THE BEST CRYSTALS, METALS, AND GEMS TO WEAR OR CARRY

Jewelry you already own will already be filled with your own power. You may have one or two really precious pieces you have been given by family or a boyfriend/girlfriend. But you can also buy relatively cheap bracelets and crystal pendants if you want a particular color and/or type for your magick. You can then wear the empowered jewelry to radiate its energies.

If you don't want to use precious gems or metals, you can use ordinary polished crystals or metal-colored tokens. After you fill them with magick, you can carry them in a small drawstring bag or purse where you can hold or touch them when you need energy or protection. Or you can hide your bag in your bedroom for safekeeping. You can also keep a small crystal in a bag with your computer or tablet or smartphone, as some crystals, like turquoise or malachite, protect against theft and damage.

HOW TO FILL YOUR CRYSTALS, GEMS, AND METALS WITH MAGICK

Enchant a crystal or piece of jewelry the same way you would fragrances (see **PAGES 46–47**) with your hands or wand, or hold it in your cupped hands and say what you are empowering it for, then toss it in the air nine times while saying the words faster and faster and tossing faster until, with the final toss and call of the words, you release the power in it.

If for love, reconciliation, or healing, do the same as in the method above, but slow the movements and words until you stop speaking. Gently press the crystal or piece of jewelry with your index finger, or gently touch it with your wand.

Write words for a wish over it or draw your astrological sign or a magickal symbol over it in incense stick smoke, three, six, seven, or nine times, all magickal numbers. You can find these astrological symbols on **PAGES 40–43** and **62–68** and magickal symbols on **PAGES 96–101**.

Either release the power by moving and/or speaking faster or

> ✳ TIP:
> You can use a crystal of the same color if you can't get the type listed here, or a clear sparkling quartz for anything where you need energy or power or to attract good things, or purple amethyst to calm or protect.

slower according to whether the crystal is gentle or vibrant and also depending upon the spell purpose.

COMMON GEMS AND CRYSTALS
AND THEIR MAGICKAL MEANINGS

Purple amethyst for balance and for peace

• reduce stress, panic, and worry • get rid of phobias, cravings, and fears • banish spooks • healing • communication with angels (see also clear and rose quartz) • creative inspiration • prevent nightmares • prevent insomnia •

Green- and silver-flecked aventurine for good luck and for lasting love

• protects against accidents and falls while doing sports (also carnelian) or traveling • finding a faithful boyfriend/girlfriend or new best friend • getting a place on a team or as a cheerleader • living happily in two homes if your parents are separated • liking yourself as you are and as you look •

Orange carnelian for independence and for popularity

• being accepted by people with whom you want to be friends • starting a new activity • moving away to college or into your first apartment • getting votes in a contest • more freedom from overprotective parents or caretakers • if you are teased or worry about your looks or image •

Yellow citrine for learning fast and for getting rid of spite and teasing

• having fun • study and learning • giving talks • presentations and assignments • technological wizardry • luck in money-making schemes • successful bidding on eBay • starting a business at a young age • protection against liars, gossip, spite, and human snakes on- and offline • exercise and fitness programs, adventures • finding what you lost •

Clear crystal quartz for getting what you want

• happiness if you are sad • making new friends if you are shy or moving to a new place • getting top marks • a big opportunity if there is lots of competition • success in anything • wishes • keeping away ghosts and fears at night or your friends are messing around with Ouija boards •

Red jasper for courage and for change

• protects against bullies and online trolls • sports success and winning competitions • whenever you are scared • guarding against aggressive people and danger • finishing homework assignments or projects on time • when you really like someone but they don't notice you •

Blue and gold lapis lazuli for success and for leadership

• faithful love • loyal friends • to come first if there is competition • getting voted to a leadership position • good school reports • success in driving tests, examinations, and interviews • against lies, unfairness, or favoritism • to guard against envy and jealousy • being accepted at the best high school, college, internship, training program, or apprenticeship • being heard in custody battles over you • overcoming major anxiety or fears •

Bright green-and-black malachite for saying no and for overcoming fears

• stopping people from using you • banishing friends or a boyfriend/girlfriend who drains your energy and makes you feel dumb •

keeping near computer, tablet, and smartphone to guard against online abuse • spite • social media attacks and trolls • overcoming fears of flying, depression, anxiety, and phobias • buying and selling on eBay • to get the right vacation or weekend job •

Shimmering white moonstone, crystal of the moon, for romance and to keep away nightmares

• helping younger women move into harmony with their bodily cycles • to give men hormonal balance • discovering and keeping secrets • protection while traveling to school or work • mending quarrels with friends or keeping the peace with warring parents • holidays across the ocean • moon magick •

Pink rose quartz for all love and for mending quarrels

• if people are leaving you out of activities • new friendship, first love, and rebuilding trust • increasing your beauty, radiance, and charisma • happy family and home • healthy and happy pets • get-togethers • pajama parties, bachelorette parties, and sleepovers • peaceful sleep and beautiful dreams • overcoming past hurt, neglect, or abuse • contacting angels and fairies •

Smoky quartz or Apache tear (obsidian) for light at the end of the tunnel

• getting better if you or a family member are ill or depressed • reduces anxiety, insomnia, nightmares, thoughts of self-harm, and panic • keep with your computer, tablet, or smartphone to prevent theft, damage, and accidents • guards against ghosts and friends who call up spirits to scare you • for learning to drive a car, scooter, or motorcycle • for safety when traveling •

Golden tiger's eye for reflecting back jealousy and spite, and for attracting opportunities

• good luck • attracting praise and prizes • getting the right sports or study scholarship • money if you are always broke • driving away all who wish you harm (a good anti–evil eye crystal) • seeing through false friends • overcoming cliques or rivalry • the chance to do well in any performance, audition, reality show, or team event •

PRECIOUS GEMS

If you have been given a special ring or pendant as a present, this will be filled with love, especially if it has been in the family for a while. Even a tiny gem holds incredible power.

Sparkling clear diamond for radiance and for enchantment

• making you feel radiant and lovely • faithful love • protects against jealousy, spite, and evil spirits • powerful against those who try to break up families and friendships •

Green emerald for lasting love and for granting wishes

• overcoming prejudice and inequality in families, religion, or culture where women are regarded as second-class citizens • prevents mind games and attacks by bad spirits, especially at night • loyalty in all relationships •

Red ruby for faithfulness and mending quarrels or separations

• love with someone who is a bit older than you • faithful love • heals sorrow • bringing together families who are apart or if a boyfriend/girlfriend, best friend, or parent has let you down •

against spirit attack • people who lie about you • brings happy
psychic dreams • a future wealth crystal •

Sapphire for truth and fair treatment in all matters

• love, faithfulness • overcomes injustice, especially by powerful
or aggressive people • reveals truth when you are being told lies
• connection with the angels and spirit guardians • good luck •
increasing magickal powers •

MAGICK METALS

Wear your metals as part of a pendant or as a bracelet, necklace, belt
buckle, or ring.

Copper, metal of Venus, for making friends and for banishing shyness

• stops homesickness • helps you to mix at parties and social
events • a copper ring on the left ring finger for calling love • on
the right ring finger for calling new friends into your life • travel
sickness • good for bringing suppleness and fitness in exercise
and sports •

Gold, metal of the Sun, for big ambitions and major success

• gold jewelry for success • saving and making money for a
major item like a car, a new smartphone, or your college fund
• gold charms for standing out from the crowd at interviews or
auditions • the smallest piece of real gold to make you look and
feel a million dollars •

Silver, metal of the Moon, for psychic powers and beautiful dreams

• silver chains, rings, or bracelets for reducing fears about your
appearance if others tease you • new and first love, or love
and friendship where family disapproves of your boyfriend/

girlfriend/friends • traveling at night • good luck as silver charms • guards against nightmares, spook attacks, threats of demons, or curses by so-called friends •

Stainless steel, metal of Mars, to reflect back all bad vibes and for strength in the way you need it

• polished steel as a pendant or item in your workspace to reflect back jealousy, spite, and nastiness • gives courage to out-face anyone who constantly criticizes or picks on you • removes bad habits • attracts luck • gives charisma and popularity •

BIRTHSTONES

Each zodiac sign has its own birthstone; the following are the most usual associations. You can give your lucky birthstone further power by drawing your zodiac sign over it with your index finger or the smoke of an incense stick. You can do this both during your zodiac period and any time when you feel afraid or anxious or you need a sudden rush of confidence. You can also light your zodiac candle color next to it.

**Aries, the Ram,
March 21–April 20, red**
Diamond, red jasper, orange
carnelian, blood agate, red tiger's eye

**Taurus, the Bull,
April 21–May 21, pink or green**
Emerald, rose quartz, jade,
chrysoprase, green or pink calcite

Gemini, the Heavenly Twins,
May 22–June 21, yellow or pale gray
Opal, citrine, labradorite, yellow
calcite, agate, yellow jasper,
alexandrite

Cancer, the Crab,
June 22–July 22, silver
Pearl, moonstone, selenite, satin
spar, clear topaz, white coral,
cloudy or milky white quartz

Leo, the Lion,
July 23–August 23, gold
Ruby, amber, red spinel, white
sapphire, sardonyx, sunstone

Virgo, the Maiden,
August 24–September 22,
pale green
Green garnet, peridot, jade,
white howlite, moss or tree agate,
serpentine, green calcite

Libra, the Scales,
September 23–October 23, blue
Sapphire, white or rainbow
opal, lapis lazuli, blue lace agate,
blue quartz

Scorpio, the Scorpion,
October 24–November 22,
indigo or dark red

Black pearl, black opal, coral,
obsidian, malachite, red spinel,
hematite

Sagittarius, the Archer,
November–23 December 21,
orange, bright yellow, or
turquoise

Orange aragonite, azurite,
chrysocolla, blue goldstone and
goldstone, blue howlite, clear
quartz, golden topaz, yellow
jasper, zircon

Capricorn, the Goat,
December 22–January 20,
brown or very dark purple

Red garnet, green aventurine,
bronzite, smoky quartz,
rubellite, tiger's eye, onyx

Aquarius, the Water Bearer,
January 21–February 18,
purple or dark blue

Amethyst, angelite, sodalite,
blue quartz, Andean blue
opal, sugilite

Pisces, the Fish
February 19–March 20,
soft white, cream, or mauve

Aquamarine, clear quartz, fluorite,
clear aragonite, aquamarine,
mother-of-pearl

MAKING CRYSTAL CHARM BAGS

All charm bags contain three, five, seven, or nine natural items in a drawstring bag or purse of the right color, unless they are for love, where you have a matching pair. The number of items in a charm bag are traditional and seem to work well. But if they don't feel right, put in as many or as few as you want. Crystal shops, bargain stores, and online stores all sell small drawstring bags in different colors at good prices.

You can use different crystals with similar meanings, or make a bag of crystals with a combination of the different powers you need to make up your magick message. Or use the same kind of crystals for a concentrated spell.

Empower or enchant your crystal bag with a spell, or put the crystals on the bag and wave incense smoke around your bag and wish for any special goals or any powers you are hoping to gain.

Crystal mixes that work well in charm bags for different needs

Here are more crystals you can use for some of the crystal mixes. They are ones you can easily buy and are especially good for the purposes suggested below. But if you can't find them, use the list in this chapter and replace with one of the same color.

For good luck: Use three green aventurine crystals in a green bag.

For meeting a new love or increasing existing love: Two matching pink rose quartz hearts in a pink bag; add a blue lapis for lasting faithfulness if, for example, you are going to different colleges.

For protection if someone is giving you a hard time: Use red, orange, yellow, blue, and gray crystals, or a black crystal in a red bag.

To help you shine in every way: Add red, orange, yellow, green, blue, purple, and clear crystals to a white bag.

To pass tests or examinations or to shine well in interviews or auditions: Add a blue and gold lapis lazuli, a green aventurine, your own birth crystal or gem, a yellow citrine, and clear quartz to a blue bag.

For safe and happy travel: Add blue aventurine, falcon's eye (blue or green tiger's eye), green jade, pink or purple kunzite, and turquoise to a green or yellow bag.

For getting money in a hurry for a special trip or something you urgently need: Add a yellow citrine, a green jade, red tiger's eye, and a golden tiger's eye and any goldstone (blue or orange) in a yellow bag.

For happiness at home if there have been a lot of quarrels: Add a purple amethyst, a brown- or gray-banded agate, and a rose quartz to a pink bag.

For introducing a new pet or settling an existing one who is unhappy or unwell: Add a brown-banded agate; a black tourmaline or jet; a gray smoky quartz; and a green and white tree or dendritic agate to a brown bag.

CHAPTER 7
✳ MAGICK WITH FLOWERS ✳

It's wonderful to get flowers from our beloved with a romantic message. You can also buy them for your best friend, your mom, or anyone special to you and say, "Three by three, magick return as sweet flowers to me."

You can use flowers from the garden or from a shopping mall. You can buy scented candles, potpourri, or flower waters. Use floral bath products in a candlelit fragrant bath. You can enchant your favorite fragrance, too. Flowers added to spells bring happiness, beauty and radiance, good fortune, and love.

> ✳ TIP: What you send out magickally, good or bad, returns to you three times as powerfully. This is called the Law of Three.

ENCHANTING FLOWERS, FLORAL BATH PRODUCTS, FLOWER WATERS, AND FRAGRANCES

So, let's start our fragrant, flower-strewn path with enchantment. Remember the fairy stories filled with enchanted forests and enchanted castles? That is pretty standard magick, actually.

Enchanting your favorite fragrance spray or bath oil can make a first date special. If you give some flowers you have enchanted to your mom, it will help her if she is feeling unloved and over it all. She might even invite your dad out on a date!

You can also enchant just about anything, from your favorite jewelry to a mug of herbal tea or a smoothie you make for someone you want to fancy you or for yourself if you are stressed and need to chill. We are going to practice enchantment using our hands and a wand.

✳ Note: There are many witches who believe it is wrong to practice on someone in any way without their permission, and it's up to each witch to find where they stand on this.

THE RITUAL
How to Enchant a Fragrance or Whatever You Wish

Just follow these simple steps. The actions are ones you have met in spellcasting, and of course you can make enchantment part of a spell or ritual if you want. The more you work with magick, the more words and actions can take on the form of a spell.

1. Pass your writing hand clockwise a few inches above your flowers, bath product, or fragrance spray, palms down and fingers together. Pass your other hand counterclockwise at

the same time over the fragrance, or spiral your wand in your writing hand and the other hand counterclockwise at the same time.

2. This time, instead of building up the power faster and faster as we did when casting spells, we are going to do the opposite to promote calm and peace.

3. Say the same magick words over and over again, for example, *"I fill this fragrance/these flowers with enchantment, that from this hour they will bring magickal power."*

4. Speak more and more slowly while moving your hands slowly and then gradually slow them down and speak more softly until you are silent and your hands are still.

5. Then push down with your index fingers or wand onto the flowers or whatever you are enchanting.

6. Then spray on the fragrance or have a scented bath and—wow!

USING ENCHANTMENT IN THE EVERYDAY WORLD

This method can be used in many ways, both as specific spells and by enchanting potpourri, flower petals, or scented candles, or even in cooking to lift the mood. Here are some ways to use enchanted florals:

*   If everyone is bad-tempered at home, enchant a bowl of potpourri and leave it in the room where everyone is supposed to relax.

*   Enchant candles before a party to make everyone have a good time.

*   Fill a small bag or purse with dried rose petals or lavender heads. Open lavender, chamomile, or rosehip tea bags if you

can't get the pure flowers, and enchant it to give you confidence if you have to face a superior clique keeping you out of the cheer squad when you know you are better than any of them.

* Add enchanted sugar violets or rose essence to a special cake to make you extra persuasive if you want your dad to increase your allowance.

* Practice enchantment and you'll soon get the rhythm and knock the socks off those storybook fairy queens.

THE MAGICKAL MEANINGS OF FLOWERS

Each flower has its own magickal meaning, and you can enchant a bouquet of flowers, a handful of flower petals, or a pot of potpourri. You can even use different flowers in a mini bouquet to send a magickal message or to create a wish for yourself on your altar. Use a combination of flowers from the list below, or get a book on the Victorian language of flowers to send a secret message. If you want, you can add a card saying what each flower means if you are sending it to someone special. If you want to grow your own magickal garden, go to the garden center and get a few flowers to plant or put in a pot. Flower petals are also great for making circles outdoors.

* TIP: You can also create your own enchantment spells using flower scents in bath products. These products often contain several different flowers or herbs that can make your magickal wishes come true.

Apple blossom

• Health • love • romance • good luck • sticking with study or training if success seems far away • hope and energy if you feel depressed, sleepy or anxious •

Carnation (red)

• For a hot date or romance • calling back a love who has left you • to give to your mom •

Carnation, (white)

• If a pet dies • overcoming rivalry from brothers and sisters • for remembering family members who have died •

Carnation (yellow)

• To stop spite, gossip, and people always criticizing you •

Chrysanthemum (brown)

• Ending love or friendship that has gone wrong • healing pets • feeling safe after a bad experience •

Chrysanthemum (red)

• For lasting love and maybe a ring • making a boyfriend/girlfriend more exciting •

Chrysanthemum (white)

• For truth in love and friendship if you suspect someone is lying • for calming down if people are hassling you •

Crocus

• Happiness • new love • to give to your love on Valentine's Day • planning the future with your boyfriend/girlfriend •

Cyclamen

• Protection • especially psychic protection against bad magick and ghosts • being made to feel special and pampered •

Daffodil

• Forgiveness • finding your true love • starting again when things go wrong •

Daisy (Michaelmas)

• If you are being unfairly accused or blamed at home, school, or by neighbors •

Fern (fragrant as incense)

• Protection • luck • unexpected money or gifts • looking good if you worry about your appearance or image • increasing fitness • travel opportunities •

Forget-me-not

• If your love is now with someone else and you still love them • improving your memory for an examination, test, or assignment •

Freesia

• For increasing trust in love and friendship • inner beauty so others admire you • saying no to someone who is pressuring you to have sex if you don't want to • enthusiasm for life •

Gardenia

• Increasing your beauty and popularity • fun and parties •

Geranium

• Overcoming shyness and teasing • happiness with family and reunions with old friends both online or offline •

Heather

• Good luck • wish magick • loyalty in love and friendship • when your love is going away • for money-earning chances •

Hibiscus

• Romance with the right person • skill in psychic powers • self-esteem and loving yourself as you are •

Honeysuckle

Money through luck • psychic powers • protection from those who tell lies •

Hyacinth

• Family love and a happy home • mending quarrels •

Ivy (fragrant as incense)

• Protection • not being torn in half if parents separate • to overcome overpossessive parents, friends, or a boyfriend/girlfriend who gets jealous •

Jasmine

Romance • moon magick • wishes • beautiful dreams • protection against ghosts •

Lavender

Love • protection against spite or cruelty • quiet sleep • happiness and peace • for remembering past lives (especially in dreams) • getting rid of fears and anxieties •

Lilac

• Happiness at home and healing quarrels with family • for happy get-togethers • connecting with old friends and past loves •

Lily

• Stopping people trying to break up your relationship • keeping

away love rivals • peace if you are surrounded by noisy people • good if you have Asperger's, autism, or ADHD •

Lily of the valley

• Increases memory and concentration for homework • takes away pressures of study • gentle love if you are scared • the return of happiness • for getting someone to listen to you •

Lotus, also orchid

Love and passion • remembering past lives • increasing psychic powers • beauty and inner radiance that get you noticed • uncovering secrets • for secret love • for celebrity, media, or modeling opportunities • for competing •

Marigold

• Protection against nasty people • overcoming problems with the law and authority • increases psychic powers • lets love grow and last •

Mimosa

• Protection • loyalty in love • past worlds and astral travel in sleep • making new good friends • travel •

Orange blossom

• Love • especially long-term love • feeling good about yourself • attracting money and what you really want • good luck • success in examinations, tests, and interviews • for power and energy •

Passionflower

• Loyalty in love and hot dates • stops nightmares • friendships • love forever • for energy day and night •

Rose (the best love flower)

• Love and love magick • enchantment • psychic powers • brings good fortune and money • happy vacations • beauty • charisma • self-image and radiance •

Violet

• Keeping secrets • secret love • uncovering hidden talents • new love and trust •

MAGICKAL FLORAL BATHS OR SHOWERS

Now that you know how to enchant your special fragrance and bath products so they are filled with power, you can make your bath or shower a special magickal experience to bring their powers into your life. You can choose what you enchant them for.

Start by putting soft lighting around the outside of the bathtub or shower. Choose a bath fragrance containing the flowers that bring what you most desire. In the evening, you can light rose- or lavender-scented candles or pink or purple tealights in deep holders on safe surfaces around the bathroom. Gently rub the fragrance into your body with a washcloth. Whether you are having a bath or shower, keep moving the fragrant cloth in gentle spirals over your body. Imagine swimming deep in the sea with rainbow fish or under a gentle waterfall. Picture yourself totally relaxed, radiant, and wherever and whomever you want to be.

Play soft music, not rock 'n' roll, and make sure you get some undisturbed time if you share a bathroom with family or roommates.

Swirl soap bubbles so they catch the candlelight. Push the bubbles toward you as you make wishes to attract what or whom you most want or what you would like to become. Push away bubbles with your hands to remove any doubts, fears, negative people, or unhappiness.

✳ TIP: If you need energy, want to lift sadness or depression, or get the morning moving, choose flowers in your bath/shower products that give you power and energy, and let natural light filter through if your bathroom has windows.

If in the shower, you can draw bubbles in your hands to cover your heart area to attract positive powers and confidence. To remove what you don't want from your life, collect bubbles in your hands and flick them to the side of the shower curtain.

You can, if you want, add rhyming words over and over during this relaxing form of bathing magick. These would call any special needs as part of your magickal bath or shower.

Are these now spells? In a sense, yes, but you can make magick anywhere, anytime, without an altar or magickal tools. Just say words and do actions with whatever you have at hand, in this case with your fragrance bubbles.

Take magick out of a set spellcasting place and time. Then it instantly becomes what it has always been to ordinary folk—a way of making the right things happen in your daily world.

✳ TIP: Always check unfamiliar bath and shower products on a small area of skin to make sure you are not allergic.

CHAPTER 8

✳ CANDLE MAGICK ✳

Candles are the simplest and yet probably the most instant and powerful magick, since just by lighting them, you release their magickal energies. By the time the candle has burned down, you will have created a lot of magickal oomph.

You can mark the unlit wax with magick words or with your zodiac sign and the sign of anyone else you are casting a spell for using your athame or a candle-carving tool. See **CHAPTER 12** to learn about magickal signs and symbols.

If you want to spread the light when sending love or healing, you should blow out the candle flame at the end of the spell. If you want to take away fear or anything bad in your life, you should extinguish the candle with a candlesnuffer (get one for your treasure box from a gift store or online) or with the back of a spoon (not your fingers, as you can give yourself a nasty burn).

Even if drop-dead gorgeous firefighters arrive, that won't make burning the house down any better in your parents' eyes. So please be careful when using candles.

Never leave candles alight when you are not there, and never leave burning candles near fabrics, clothes, curtains, pets, or small children. If the spell says leave the candle to burn and you have to go out or to sleep, blow it out and relight to finish burning another time.

Stand candles in or on heatproof containers, especially beeswax candles or if you are melting wax for images. You can always buy a sheet of beeswax from a craft store or online and warm it to melt with a hair dryer.

When burning wishes, always drop the paper into a deep pot of sand or soil *before* it sets properly alight. Sand or soil are best to extinguish an overburning candle (never water), and with beeswax, exercise extra care as it can spit, especially if homemade.

BURNING CANDLE WISHES

If you burn written wishes in a candleflame, you are doubling the power of the candleflame and releasing the wish with a whoosh into the cosmos—this is *really* powerful magick!

1. Begin by writing your wish on a thin piece of paper, about nine inches long, in the color of the candle you are going to burn, chosen from the list of colors in **CHAPTER 5** or on

white paper in blue or black ink. As you write the wish, say it aloud.

2. When you have finished, fold up the paper into a taper shape, narrowed at one end.

3. Light a large candle in the color of your wish in the center of your altar, placing a large fireproof plate or tray under the candleholder, and have a pot of soil or sand nearby.

4. Hold the narrowed end of the paper downward into the candle flame and singe it, dropping it fast into the pot of soil as it begins to burn.

5. Let the paper burn away in the pot and bury the ashes under a flowering or green plant.

ANOINTING CANDLES WITH OIL

Anointing is the witch word for rubbing oil into the wax of an unlit candle to fill it with extra power.

Remember to write any words or zodiac signs on candles with your athame or your finger (using the index finger of the hand you write with on the unlit wax) before anointing your candle. You can also draw images on the candles. In **CHAPTER 12,** which is about secret signs, you will find magickal images you can draw, either invisibly or with your athame, on your candle and release the power when lighting.

As you rub oil into your wish candle, repeat your wish softly and continuously. For example, if you are lighting a golden-brown candle for money, to get a car, or for the latest smartphone, you might say, "Candle bright, with your light, bring me the money soon/by the next moon for my new (object of desire)."

Use a small bowl of pure

✳ **Warning:** Anointed candles are more flammable than regular candles, so put the oil on while they are unlit, and use a large metal tray underneath them when burning. Don't get oil on or too near the wick.

extra virgin olive oil from the kitchen cupboard. You can anoint candles for every kind of magick no matter the spell. This is because the oil adds power to the fire and brightness of the candle, whatever the spell is for.

Rub the oil with the index finger of your writing hand down the wax of the unlit candle from the top but not around the wick area, holding the candle firmly with the other hand, covering all sides.

Stop just below halfway down the candle and then rub from the bottom upward with the same index finger, again naming the purpose.

Work to just above halfway so the rubbed-in oil overlaps in the middle.

Light the candle.

MAKING MAGICK CHARMS WITH BEESWAX CANDLES

Before you begin, remember that you *must* keep to the most important magick rule: harm no one by magick, even if they are a bad person. You can banish or block their bad behavior, but you can't, despite what you see in popular culture, actually turn your boyfriend or girlfriend into a toad; you can only let the world see them for the toad they really are.

Beeswax candles melt fast and so are ideal for making charms. Light the candle on a broad flat candleholder or on an old heatproof flat metal dish or tray so the melting wax will spread. If you are using a tray, light the candle in advance and drip some wax onto it to help the candle stick to it. Blow out the candle to keep it ready for the ritual later. You can use the resulting pool of melted wax for making lucky or protective charms or tiny figures for love.

You can do this as part of a spell or make the beeswax-candle lighting and the creation of the charm the entire spell.

If this is the whole spell, name what you are lighting the candle for.

Once it is burned, draw an image in the cooling fallen wax with your athame or write two or three words for what it is you most need or desire.

✳ **TIP:** You shouldn't anoint candles you are making charms from as it spoils the consistency of the wax. Since beeswax candles are pretty flammable, it is an extra safety hazard.

Cut a circle around the image or words and ease the cooled wax off the tray with a spatula. Keep the image in a cloth bag. When it crumbles, bury it under a flowering plant to return the energies to Mother Earth.

USING SYMBOLS WITH YOUR CANDLES

If you use soft wax candles or beeswax, you can press different crystals near the bottom of your candle. You could instead press in coins for money. The power of the crystal or coin is set free into your life once the candle has burned enough for the coin or crystal to fall out. You can go back to **PAGES 35–38** to remind yourself of the magickal powers of each crystal. The crystal or coin then becomes a powerful lucky talisman.

CHAPTER 9

✳ ASTROLOGICAL MAGICK ✳

All witches are natural astrologers. Before long you will be advising your friends on their astrological love and friendship compatibilities and what they really want to do with their lives.

Candles are the single best way of working with all kinds of astrological magick.

Each zodiac sign represents special strengths (see **PAGES 62-68**) that you can call upon in spellwork. So, if it's all about wanting a special trip, you can use Gemini yellow or Sagittarius turquoise candles with that glyph scratched on them to call it into your life. In candle magick you can borrow these powers whenever you need a particular zodiac strength in your life, even if it is not your own birth sign, symbol, and color.

However, keep in mind that this will only work if it is meant to be. Magick in all its forms opens up our own attracting energies so we are much more positively visible. It also draws us like a magnet at the right time to the right place and the right person or opportunity. I have come across people who have lit astrology candles to attract one person but a different person comes along, and it's just right.

ASTROLOGY CANDLES—THE LOWDOWN

How to prepare your astrology candles for magick:

1. Scratch or etch your own zodiac sign onto a candle in your personal zodiac color (listed below) using your athame, or invisibly using the index finger of your writing hand.

2. Light that candle, which now magickally bears your zodiac sign, to make any candle magick more powerful.

3. After you light your personal zodiac candle, put a pinch of salt in the flame to make it sparkle any time you need to feel more confident.

First let's learn the right glyphs or signs, the dates, and the candle colors.

The following list not only gives you your personal zodiac sign and candle color, but the strengths you can borrow from any of the signs at any time to make your spells work really well.

Aries, the Ram,
for courage and for positive
competitiveness
(March 21–April 20), red

• making yourself heard if you are shy
• new ideas and beginnings • standing up to bullies • activities, sports, and getting fit •

Taurus, the Bull,
for self-confidence and mental
toughness
(April 21–May 21), pink or green
• letting your natural attractiveness
shine through • removing zits and
blemishes • patience when things
are stuck • beating anxiety in new
situations or when with new people •

Gemini, the Heavenly Twins, for
learning new things and for adapting
to any situation or opportunity (May
22–June 21), yellow or pale gray
• speaking and writing clearly and
confidently • new opportunities and
activities • weekends away with
friends or your significant other •
happy summer camps • dealing with
pesky brothers and sisters • passing
your driving test • getting accepted
for an action-packed career •

Cancer, the Crab,
for happiness at home and for
mending quarrels
(June 22–July 22), silver

• Happy family life • for mothers • new
and growing love • rebuilding trust if
you have been hurt • keeping secrets
and secret love • getting in touch with
your body • making wishes on the
crescent and full moon •

Leo, the Lion,
for leadership and for taking
center stage in life
(July 23–August 23), gold

• standing out from the crowd •
popularity • fame and fortune • fun
• parties and celebrations • lasting
faithful love • major success in every
way • performances • father with
children •

Virgo, the Maiden, for fixing people's problems and for good health (August 24–September 22), pale green

• organizing yourself, your work, and your studies better • paying more attention to detail • bringing order out of chaos • tidying your room • exercise and fitness • time outdoors • healing gifts •

Libra, the Scales, for keeping the peace and for seeing both sides of the argument (September 23–October 23), blue

• fairness if you are being badly treated, excluded from cliques, or unfairly blamed at home • standing up for justice • dealing with authority, the law, and parental custody disputes • making lots of friends • natural charm and charisma •

Scorpio, the Scorpion,
for strong feelings and for defeating
lies, spite, and gossip
(October 24–November 22), indigo
or dark red

• increasing your psychic powers
• growing closeness with an
undemonstrative partner or family
member • discovering secrets •
overcoming very strict parents or
community • getting back what has
been taken from you • protection
against evil spirits •

Sagittarius, the Archer,
for long-distance travel and for
opening up new opportunities
(November 23–December 21),
orange, bright yellow, or turquoise

• feeling hopeful if you are sad or
lonely when alone • house moves
• adventures • writing and creative
activities • trying new things •
discovering the truth • aiming for
what seems an impossible goal •
camping, trekking, and backpacking •

Capricorn, the Goat,
for going step-by-step to what you want, for being careful with money, and for whom you trust (December 22–January 20), brown or very dark purple

• watching what you say if you are in a tricky situation • for achieving ambitions when there is a lot of study or training involved • following rules when you have no choice • protection against danger • attracting money •

Aquarius, the Water-carrier,
for independence and for good friendships (January 21–February 18), purple or dark blue

• if your family is overprotective • new friendships and joining friendship and social groups • protection on social media • solving long-standing problems • resisting emotional blackmail and overpossessiveness • doing charity work and raising money for charity •

Pisces, the Fish, for trusting your intuition and for multitasking (February 19–March 20), soft white, cream, or mauve

• fulfilling secret dreams • understanding other people whose points of view are different • following two interests or study programs at the same time • accepting and being accepted by new family members such as stepparents, stepbrothers, or stepsisters • for living in two households • success in all water sports or activities • safety in spiritual activities •

USING YOUR ASTROLOGICAL CANDLES FOR A MAGICKAL PARTY WITH YOUR FRIENDS

This is a seriously fun social event, and if you do it monthly, you and your friends can take turns organizing it and deciding who is bringing the candles and providing snacks. You can also take turns leading the ritual. You might have a joint money pot so no one has to spend too much out of their own pocket.

Though this ritual is often done on the crescent moon, you can have an astrological candle party with your friends any time of the month. This can also be one of your full moon activities if you organize a regular magick group (see **CHAPTER 13**).

Each person present will need two candles. The first is their own personal astrological candle color, and the second astrological candle color should represent their wish, such as red (Aries) for courage if they are being bullied and want it to stop. Send everyone the zodiac signs and color meanings in advance to help you out.

Go to a garage sale or thrift store to buy deep heatproof candleholders so everyone present can have two, or ask people to bring their own holders.

Everyone should sit in a circle with their two candles in front of them. Surround the candles with jewelry, coins, fruits, flowers, and any symbols that will bring good things specific to the wish, like a silver horseshoe for luck or a toy car if you are saving for a car. You will want to remind the group ahead of time to bring these items, but the host should have lots of spare items in a box in case someone forgets.

Each person writes their own astrological glyph on the side of their own astrological color candle and the astrological sign of what they wish for on the second candle. Do this invisibly with the index finger of the writing hand. You can also use long sewing pins, a letter opener, a candle-carving tool, or your athame to scratch the signs into the unlit candles more easily.

In the middle of the circle the leader, sometimes called the High Priest/ess, lights a big silver moon candle pushed into a deep heatproof pot of sand or soil, saying, "Welcome to this moon rite. May the angels guard us through this eve and till morning light."

The leader of the rite lights her zodiac birth candle from the silver candle, then lights the first person's birth candle in the circle.

Then each person in the circle lights the next person's zodiac birth candle from theirs, moving clockwise around the circle.

Afterward, when all the personal zodiac candles are lit, the leader lights her zodiac wish candle from the silver one. She lights the first person's wish candle in the circle. Then each person lights the wish candle of the person to their left, again moving clockwise around the circle.

Each person blows softly three times into their zodiac birth sign candle at a prearranged signal from the leader, who can sit in the middle of the circle if preferred, and then each does the same for the wish candle.

Each person in turn says, "I wish for . . ." (and says silently or aloud the actual wish) speaking around the circle.

Each person speaking around the circle can also in turn name a person, animal, or place in need of healing.

Afterward, the leader says, "We send blessings and light to all and ask that our wishes are granted in the way and time that is right to be. Blessings be on all."

All repeat together, "Blessings be on all," then blow out their candles at the same time. The central one is left burning while you all enjoy food and music.

If you are working alone, you can light zodiac candles for people you care for and burn wishes for each of them in your central flame.

CHAPTER 10

❄ MOON MAGICK ❄

Magick has been practiced under the full moon for hundreds of years. If you start your own magick group (see **PAGES 102–108**) you may decide to meet on a full moon night, called an Esbat, as well as during other phases of the moon.

LIVING WITH THE PHASES OF THE MOON

Becoming aware of the cycles of the moon results in smoother-flowing days, calmer evenings, and sweet-dream nights. Once your hormones kick in, right through until you are old, moon phases affect your moods, words, and actions.

As the moon waxes or grows you will find you have more energy than at other moon times. You can use this time for trying new kinds of exercise (maybe even extreme sports), organizing a party, or planning a fun weekend with your friends. Then as the moon wanes or gets smaller in size and power, you may feel you want to get more rest and enjoy quieter activities such as walking or swimming, mellow catch-up coffee dates, or romantic candlelit evenings.

You can follow the moon phases online. Make sure you choose a site that shows your own time zone. If you prefer, buy a moon diary that has the moon times for your region. This will tell you what the moon is doing in the sky each night and when the all-powerful full moons are.

Always remember, however, that what you see in the sky and what you feel are your best guides to using moon energies. The best way to follow the monthly journey of the moon is to keep a daily journal for a few months. You will notice how your moods and energy levels increase or decrease according to the phases of the moon. Note what you feel each day.

Over the next few months, write down if you feel unduly active or depressed without reason, and check the moon phase. You may find that particular days of the waxing or waning moon cycles affect you strongly, either positively or negatively, each month. Each of us reacts in different ways to the psychic pull of the moon.

ALL ABOUT MOON MAGICK

Moon magick is good for love and romance, especially new or first love. It also forms a focus for any wishes or worries to do with girls, women, and men who want to connect with their gentle side. Moon magick can be used for developing your psychic powers, protection while traveling at night, and bringing chances to travel, especially overseas or interstate.

It increases beauty and radiance and improves your self-image if you worry about the way you look or if others tease you about being different. Try moon magic to be noticed in a good way when you want, but to keep a low profile when you don't. Finally, moon magick can be practiced for any concerns about your mom, female relatives, and teachers or friends of any sex or gender, and secrets that can't be revealed.

ALL ABOUT THE MOON

The Moon's day:

Monday, a special day for moon magick, whatever the phase.

Color and metal:

Silver

Flowers, incenses, and herbs:

• all small, white flowers, especially fragrant ones • coconut •
eucalyptus • iris • jasmine • lemon • lemon balm • lemon verbena
• lotus • mimosa • myrrh • white lily • white sandalwood •

Angels:

• starry-robed Gabriel with a silver halo • Ofaniel, angel of the
Wheel of the Moon, who brings each new constellation into
view as it turns each month •

Crystals:

• moonstone • pearl • mother-of-pearl • pearl selenite • opal or
white or pearly seashells, especially double ones •

Remember to leave your crystals out on the full moon night or the
night before or after to recharge them with energy and wash away any
psychic garbage.

THE THREE PHASES OF THE MOON

The main three phases are linked with the three stages of the Goddess:
Maiden (waxing or growing), Mother (full), and Wise woman (waning).

The waxing phase begins when the crescent moon is first seen in
the sky on day 3 or 4 of the moon cycle until the night of the full moon.
Full moon energies start a day or two before the actual full moon and

end a day or two after. The waning phase comes after the full moon and extends until the moon disappears from the sky.

The crescent moon and the waxing moon are good for:

• new beginnings • working toward a long-term goal or study plan • chances to earn much needed money • attracting good luck • study and homework • being confident • becoming less shy and more popular • finding friendship, love, and romance • being included in teams and social groups • doing well in sports • increasing your psychic and magickal powers •

The full moon is good for:

• a passionate date • anything urgent • standing up to bullies • changing majors, or going to live, study, or work in a new place • traveling • protecting yourself from spirits and demons • faithfulness, commitment, and loyalty • justice if you are being unfairly treated or blamed • a big dream • overcoming rivals • examination or work success • leadership •

The waning period is good for:

• removing pain and sickness from self and others • healing pets • taking away whatever or whoever is blocking your happiness, popularity, or success • standing up against peer pressure • removing fears of failing, the dark, bad spirits, curses, and nightmares • banishing conflict • ending a relationship • discouraging stalkers • getting some privacy • getting rid of negative people •

The dark of the moon is the name given to the two and a half to three days when the moon disappears from the sky.

This occurs after the waning crescent has gone and before the crescent appears. It is sometimes called the new moon, still hidden in its cradle. The dark of the moon is not counted as a moon phase and is not generally used for magick. However, it is good for meditation and some quiet time.

GETTING IN TOUCH WITH THE FULL MOON

Let's start with the full or Mother moon, the easiest one to see and tune into magickally. Since the moon passes through each zodiac sign for two and a half days each month, the full moon will also fall in a different zodiac sign each month of the year. The zodiac sign that a full moon falls in affects the nature of that full moon and what it is good for.

Apply that knowledge about astrology from **CHAPTER 9** to how that zodiac power is going to affect moon magick. For example, a full moon falling in Aries is going to be pretty dynamic, like knight-on-a-white-charger stuff or going all out for a place on a team. One in Libra will be much calmer and more reasonable, and it is good if you have been treated unfairly.

Keep in mind, though, any full moon says go for whatever you want, all guns blazing. Just make sure you don't burn too many bridges while you are defeating dragons.

MAKING A MOON ALTAR

It can be very magickal to make a special moon altar outdoors on a full moon night if the weather is good. Of course, if you want to adapt your indoor bedroom altar, move it so you can see the moon through the open window as you face the altar. But, if you wish, you can use your bedroom altar exactly as it is for moon magick.

Invite friends for a full moon party and, if the weather is good, take over the garden. Make sure your candles are in sheltered glass holders and can't tip over. A picnic table can make a good outdoor altar, or use a square of wood on bricks that you can sit around.

For your moon altar you will need:

- ❋ a special silvery scarf or cloth to cover the altar.

- ❋ a silver candle at each corner instead of one in the middle.

- ❋ a bowl of water set in the center into which you have mixed three pinches of sea salt with your silver knife. Add moonstones to the water if you have them (three or seven).

- ❋ a bowl of white petals, also in the center.

- ❋ a lighted jasmine or myrrh incense stick (the fragrances of the moon) in each corner. You can buy special outdoor long incense sticks from a garden center, new age store, or online that you can place in the ground.

- ❋ Then the fun begins.

DRAWING DOWN THE FULL MOON

Almost every coven, magickal group, or solitary witch—people who like to practice magick alone—calls down the moon goddess to be with them and give them a message. You can call her by an ancient moon goddess name. Choose one from the following list, or maybe you already have your own.

Moon goddesses:

Andraste, the Celtic moon goddess, whose sacred animal was the hare.

Aphrodite, the ancient Greek moon and love goddess.

Artemis, Greek goddess of the hunt as well as the moon, and good for going all out for anything you want or need.

Diana, the ultimate moon goddess and mistress of magick, loved by the Romans. She is also associated with Artemis in Greek mythology.

Isis, the ancient Egyptian moon goddess of enchantment and of the sea whom, you might recall, could stop the sun.

Selene, moon goddess of lasting love and of happiness with family and friendship.

Your moon ceremony is best conducted outdoors when the full moon is shining, so wait till this happens, or practice the two nights before and after the full moon.

1. Face the moon, open your arms wide, and lift them upward as high as possible, bent at the elbow and palms flat.

2. Dance around and around the altar in ever-widening circles or in the outdoor space where you are holding your moon ritual. Move counterclockwise, called *moonwise* or *widdershins* (WIDD-r-shins), in magick the direction used in moon-magick

spells and rituals. Just so you know, clockwise movements you use in most spells and rituals are magickally called *sunwise* or *deosil* (DAY-uh-sill).

3. Continue swirling until you are dizzy, saying faster and faster as you turn, *"Lady of the Moon, Lady of the Moon, come to me, be with me, Lady of the Moon."* Then face the moon again, and you will *see* the moon rushing toward you. Of course, the rushing moon is a trick of the eye, but the effect is pretty cool.

4. Sit down on the ground or on a cushion and feel the moonlight enter you. Ask Lady Moon silently for what you most want and need and if she has any messages. You may hear them in your mind or see the messages as pictures or just *know* what the message is.

5. Splash water from the bowl on your brow, throat, and inner wrists, whispering, *"Come to me, be with me, Lady of the Moon."*

6. Leave the moon water with the crystals in it in the moonlight all night (in a sheltered place if necessary).

7. In the morning filter your moon water into small glass bottles to put in your bath or to dab on your brow, throat, and wrists whenever you do psychic work or feel afraid.

8. Scatter your petals as an offering for Lady Moon all around the altar, then thank the moon mother (name if wished) for blessings received. End the rite by saying, *"The Moon Rite is ended, blessings on all."*

MAKING A FULL MOON CEREMONY FOR FRIENDS

This makes an absolutely fabulous ceremony for a magick group. You could do the astrological candle ceremony (**PAGES 68–70**) on the night of the crescent moon and make drawing down the moon your full moon Esbat ceremony.

1. Everyone stands in a circle around the altar, leaving plenty of space to move.

2. From their place in the circle, facing the moon, they spin around and around until dizzy, saying in a chorus, *"Lady of the Moon, Lady of the Moon, come to us, be with us, Lady of the Moon."*

3. They then sit down in their original place in the circle.

4. Moving around the circle counterclockwise/moonwise, while still sitting on the ground, each person speaks aloud a message from the moon mother they heard, saw in the mind, or sensed.

5. When all have spoken, go around the circle again, each making a wish aloud in turn, for themselves or for someone in need.

6. Next, the bowl of water is passed moonwise around the circle, and each splashes water on their brow, throat, and inner wrist points in turn while whispering, *"Come to us, be with us, Lady of the Moon."*

7. Finally, pass the flower bowl around moonwise, everyone in turn scattering a few petals in front of them, thanking the moon mother for blessings received. Afterward, go to the center and say, *"The Moon Rite is ended, blessings on all."*

CHAPTER 11

✳ KITCHEN WITCH ✳

Magick started in the kitchen hundreds of years ago with stirring the cauldron, the cooking pot used for making family dinners and magick brews.

An apprentice witch's best friend is the kitchen pantry with all those amazing jars of dried herbs from the supermarket, herbal teas, and the spice rack to magickally heat up just about everything.

Each food or drink item has a magickal meaning. Absorbing the magick as we eat and drink, and cooking with loving wishes for family and friends for a happy evening, has been practiced for centuries. While you can't use your magick wand in the coffee shop without getting some pretty strange looks, you can substitute a teaspoon or coffee stirrer in a Starbucks cappuccino.

Of course, you can make herbal and spice charm bags like we did with crystals, stirring the herbs together in a bowl, chanting the magickal meanings, bringing down the mixing spoon in the middle of the bowl to push the power into the herbs, and knotting them in a bag or purse, and presto, your charm bag will attract what you want or protect you from what you don't want.

Herbal and fruit tea bags can be opened and put into charm bags or drunk as magickally empowered teas, or you can use the liquid from a brewed tea to sprinkle around precious items like your tablet, new car, skateboard, or scooter to protect them from thieves and accidents.

Herbs or spices can be stirred into recipes with a magickal wish as you cook a meal. A special cake for family, friends, or a significant other can be enchanted with rose essence or sugar violets or angelica, all oozing love as you stir the mix, using the spoon as the wand. You can even write magick wishes in icing on top of a cake or cupcakes, and then smooth down the icing before decorating so the wishes are in the cake.

Fruit and veggies are also amazingly magickal. You can dry out half a lemon or lime in salt to get rid of spite or even scratch, "Zit, zit, go away," on an onion or garlic clove and bury it.

So, let's start with a list of the magickal meanings attached to different foods, herbs, and spices. You can enchant them with words, your hands, or a wooden spoon used as a wand as you chop, mix, and stir. The chart below suggests how you can use them magickally. But remember, you can enchant any food or drink just with the words you say as you pass your hands or wand over them.

MAGICKAL HERBS AND SPICES

Angelica

Love; increasing beauty and radiance. Enchant sugared angelica as you decorate your cake, saying, *"I am irresistible and sweet to all who eat, radiant, disarming.*

Watch out guys/gals, I am Prince/ss Charming."

Basil

Protection against accidents and attacks with nasty words, psychic attack, or physical threats; good for bringing money when you are saving for something special. Plant your basil with six coins buried around the base of the plant, saying, *"Money grow, let it be so."*

Bay

Protection against harm; faithful love; loyalty between friends; brings and keeps money if you are always broke. For wishes, scratch with a pin on a dried bay leaf what you most want and drop the leaf in running water.

Cinnamon

Success against bullies; good luck, money, love, and passion. Mix in a charm bag with ginger and saffron for good luck, saying nine times fast, *"Good fortune have I none, into my life good luck shall come—and fast and let it last."*

Cloves

Protection and happiness in the home; keeping away spooks and nastiness; lasting love; hang an orange pomander over your altar, stick cloves all over it and into it, but don't let them pierce the fruit,

only the skin; roll in any spice on a plate, tie with red ribbon.

Coriander

Love; health; healing; protects property and also luggage while traveling if you put some seeds in a sachet; makes you smart; put nine in a tiny bag and glue or sew this inside your school bag.

Fennel

Travel, especially independently; protects children and animals; scatter fennel seeds outdoors and say whom you wish to protect.

Garlic

Protection against human nastiness, curses, and paranormal energies; brings better health; scratch on a garlic bulb anything you want to get rid of, from a zit to a stalking ex, and bury it.

Ginger

Love; money; success; power; taking the lead; good for travel sickness. Add to a charm bag with dried mint, rosemary, a small piece of gold like an earring or a gold coin, and a pearl or sparkling crystal, knot five times and toss it five times, saying, *"I will take the lead, I will win indeed,"* and on the sixth toss name how or what you want to lead, and say, *"This shall be so, success I'll know,"* then take the bag with you when facing competition.

Lemongrass

Repels spite and human snakes; good for moves and changes of all kinds; attracts success. Spiral a lighted lemongrass incense stick counterclockwise around a picture or written name of a person who has broken a friendship or relationship and say, *"Snakes in the grass, this wrong cannot pass, you both lied and betrayed me, I wish together you may be happy, I no longer seek your company,"* then cut up the pictures and throw away.

Licorice

Love; exciting dates; good luck in gambling; making new friends. Enchant licorice candies or strings, saying, *"Licorice spice is twice as nice when people care, so eat and share";* offer them to people you want to know better or leave in a dish at a party.

Mint

Money; love; attracting someone special; keeping away spite and gossip; protection against accidents and attack while traveling. Make a mint herbal tea, stir nine times clockwise, put it in a bottle, and sprinkle it outside the home of someone you like or near their fence, saying, *"Mint, mint, (name person), invite me through your*

front door, what walks in, you will adore," then find an excuse to call, delivering a leaflet about a game or even the local newsletter.

Parsley

Love; exciting dates; takes away bad luck and brings good fortune. Take a jar of parsley, stand on a bridge, and tip the herbs into the downstream water, saying, *"Flow to the river, flow to the sea, bad luck be changed to good luck for me."*

Pepper

Protection; banishing nasty people and spooks. When no one is at home but you, sprinkle pepper on the front doorstep and sweep it outward with a brush or broom, saying, *"Nothing bad may enter here, no one, no evil to make me fear,"* then leave the broom outside, bristles

upward, until just before the family returns home.

Peppermint

Increases psychic powers; stops people teasing you or ganging up on you. Enchant your peppermint or spearmint gum and chew when you see the bullies approaching.

Rosemary

Love; improves memory and concentration and so is good for tests and examinations; banishes depression and nightmares; enchanted rosemary creams or bath products increase radiance and give you fabulous hair.

Saffron

Love; happiness; brings good things fast; brings back money if you have spent too much. Put in a charm bag with two coins, shake it three times, and say three times, *"Gold and silver do I lack, I spent my money, please bring some back."*

Sage and Thyme

Grants wishes; improves memory and concentration; brings fairness and success in examinations, tests, and interviews or when you have to speak to a crowd. The night before interviews, exams, or driving tests, mix rosemary with sage and thyme in a blue bag, knot three times with blue thread, and say, *"Sage, rosemary, and thyme, let me perform well and success be mine."*

Salt

Health; long life; wealth; protection against human curses and paranormal influences. Mix salt in water with your ritual knife in your altar bowl three times counterclockwise and then three times clockwise. Make a cross on the surface of the water, and sprinkle the salt water around your room, saying, *"May only goodness and light stay here, all you of ill intent depart, I say depart,"* then throw the water away.

FOODS FOR HEALTH, LUCK, LOVE, AND SUCCESS

Apple and Pear

Good health; new and growing love. To encourage a boyfriend/girlfriend to be more romantic, cut an apple or pear in half and offer half to your boyfriend/girlfriend, saying in your mind, *"Fruit sweet, as s/he does eat, let him/her not hesitate, show your romance now to me, fruit sweet so beautiful love must be,"* then eat the other half.

Avocado

Inner radiance and outer beauty; attracts beautiful people and things into your life. Keep an avocado stone wrapped with a rose quartz crystal and some dried rose petals or potpourri for a day and night, then tip the avocado stone, crystal, and potpourri into a hole in the earth and scatter petals or potpourri around it on the replaced soil, saying, *"So shall my radiance grow and glow."*

Bread

Wishes; loyalty between friends and lovers; happy families; enough money if your folks are worried. Use a bread mix or make dough and on top, before baking, fashion a symbol made of the dough of what you most wish for (if you buy ready-made bread write your wish on top with a sharp knife), then eat your wish to absorb the magick.

Corn

Good luck; happy family if yours is always arguing; wishes; happy holidays; beginning new things or discovering new places. Enchant the corn before cooking with what you and those sharing the meal most want and need.

Eggs

New beginnings; getting back who or what has been lost. To overcome curses and people who have said nasty things to upset you or to get rid of bad spirits, throw an egg against a tree so it smashes, and say, *"Fair is foul and foul is fair, I toss your curse/evil in the air."*

Fig

Getting money if you are broke and need money for a trip or your allowance has run out.

Grapes

Mending quarrels, especially with a significant other; fun and parties; getting a better dorm, car, smartphone, or whatever needs upgrading. Pick a grape from a bunch, saying, *"Let our quarrels no more be, come in peace and love to me,"* then eat the grape, saying the words as you pick more until you have eaten enough.

Hazelnuts

Learning new or difficult things; long-term commitment to a career or study path; justice if you are being unfairly treated. Set a circle of nine nuts counterclockwise on your symbol dish. Each day hold and eat one nut, saying, *"May justice be done and truth be shown, liars unmasked and my innocence known."*

Honey/Maple Syrup

Friendship; unexpected money or praise; family happiness; fun days with friends or a special field trip; feeling beautiful and special; to make life seem happier if you hate doing something but must. If you hate school, spoon honey on waffles or pancakes each morning, saying in your mind nine times a rhyme such as, *"Today will be cool at school, sweet as honey, exciting, funny, no sting, but only happiness bring."*

Lemon

Getting rid of negative situations and people. If you must see horrible people add five drops of lemon juice to your water bottle, shake it five times, and keep it sealed between you and the person/people—don't drink it but tip it away at the end of the day as it will have absorbed the nastiness.

Lime

Justice; new beginnings, new places, and people; repels spite, jealousy, nasty neighbors, family members, and people who steal your ideas. Take half a lime and put it fruit-side down in a bowl of salt to bind nastiness, and when it is dried out, throw it and the salt away.

Onion

Luck; money; getting rid of what you don't want, from zits to warts to shyness or bad luck. Scratch on your onion what you want to get rid of and bury the onion with three coins.

Peach/Apricot/Mango

Makes you feel attractive and desirable; for calling whatever would make you happy into your life; for getting together with friends.

Potato/Fries

Friendship; anything that is slow to happen or you have to stay with; being nice to people who seem boring but who are kind; getting people to see things your way.

Enchant the family baked potatoes if you are trying to persuade your parents to change their minds and the fries of brothers/sisters/friends who are being annoying.

CHAPTER 12

* SECRET WITCH *

This is where the fun really starts. You will learn the secret magick that only you and your fellow witches will know about. You can draw invisible magickal symbols on just about everything using incense stick smoke or the index finger of your writing hand. For example, as you wear, an empowered pendant, you can touch it when you need some courage or extra strength, and only you know its power.

Many witches wear silver pentagrams around their necks to show their dedication to the Craft. Despite bad B movies, the pentagram isn't at all spooky or evil; the five-pointed star represents the five elements: earth, air, fire, water, and spirit. But in some communities or schools, people just don't get it or it may not be allowed. While you can wear your pentagram inside your clothes, sometimes it's easier to mark jewelry or your special possessions invisibly with the magickal sign. This way you have access to their power and protection any time.

CREATING SECRET MAGICK SYMBOLS

Before long you will be drawing invisible magickal symbols on just about everything.

Magick Symbols and Crystals

When you invisibly mark a crystal with a magickal symbol, you may notice that results seem quicker to achieve and the vibes stronger. Why? Gems and crystals are millions of years old and therefore are very powerful. Magickal symbols are also very old. When drawn invisibly on the crystals, they release their stored energy like opening a zip file on a computer. Their age combined with the magickal meaning of the crystal and the power of its color triples the magick. Magick just gets better and better the more you add to it.

Using Your Magick Name as a Symbol

Write your secret magick name with incense stick smoke (try rose or frankincense) over any pendant, bracelet, or ring that you will wear, to make you unstoppable.

* Touch the jewelry to increase your persuasive power when explaining why your assignment is two weeks late.

* Put it in front of your device to make a favorable first impression with a new social media group.

* Put it on if you've got a heap of clothes on your bed and you hate them all five minutes before going out. Say your magick name as you touch the jewelry and say, "I look great, whatever I wear."

Magick Tattoos

You can also create invisible magickal sigils on your energy points at different locations on your body using the ancient symbols in this chapter.

Choose from the symbols on **PAGES 96-101** you need most and, unlike tattoos, you can change them any time. Only you know what they say, though people will feel your new confidence and wittiness.

You can even put a magick tattoo over a zit so no one will notice it. As well as using the finger of your writing hand, you can trace magick symbols with your favorite fragrance on your pulse points, heart, throat, or third eye.

Draw your chosen symbol using the index finger of your writing hand:

* On your magickal third eye in the center of your brow to radiate confidence and protect against any power games or spooky energies.

* On your inner wrist points for your loving heart to bring popularity and make everyone you meet friendly.

* On the base of your throat to keep out hurtful words.

Picture magick power symbols around you in blue light if you feel spooked in your bedroom. If bullies are blocking your path, use an Egyptian scarab beetle symbol to give you the courage to walk straight past with your head held high. With your mind, you can zap a hammer of Thor protective symbol toward anyone threatening you, or a *don't notice me* moon symbol if you don't want to be asked a question in class. Your magick symbols are changing the energies around you that people pick up without realizing.

* Have your favorite magick symbols drawn invisibly on your smartphone or tablet cover.

* Draw them around your room on door handles, etc., in rose water or your favorite fragrance to keep your overly curious family from snooping.

* Draw symbols in bright colors and put them on the back of

furniture or under your bed (sticky labels are great for attaching magick symbols).

* Draw symbols in gold, then tie them to balloon strings or kites and fly them.

* Trace symbols in the pools of bubbles in your bath to keep you safe from spooks while you sleep.

* Trace symbols in the air over cakes you bake for a party with your friends.

* Make the shape of the symbol with a spoon on the surface as you stir your coffee or herbal tea to fill you with energy if you're half asleep.

* Draw one on the label of your hoodie, invisibly or with a permanent marker, to call to you new friends and opportunities if every door always seems to slam shut.

THE POWER OF DIFFERENT KINDS OF JEWELRY

If you go to new age stores and some jewelry stores you will often see some magickal symbols, such as the Egyptian ankh, as earrings or bracelets. These you can make doubly powerful by drawing the symbol over the actual shape.

You have already learned the astrological zodiac signs that you can draw over any jewelry. These will make your own special unique qualities shine out if you're shy or self-conscious or get teased a lot. You will find a list of planetary symbols and their meanings on PAGES 98-100.

Necklaces or pendants protect your invisible throat energy center from spiteful words and give you the power to say what you want without falling over the words.

Earrings guard your third or psychic eye in the center of your brow above and between your eyes where nasty thoughts from others enter. This also keeps you safe from spooky experiences.

Bracelets shield your sensitive loving heart and also send out *love me* vibes. This is because your inner wrist pulse points are connected to the heart. A necklace or pendant that covers your heart does the same.

Rings are often given in love by family, some passed down through the generations. Rings from ancestors carry the loving guardianship of family. Because rings are a perfect enclosing circle with no beginning or end, they both protect you from all harm and draw happiness and good luck. Fingers are linked with the heart energy center. A friendship or love ring worn on your heart/wedding finger is especially fortunate.

A belt protects your inner sun center at the base of your rib cage. It gives you power and confidence.

Ankle bracelets and toe rings offer defense against physical threats or danger. They send out *don't mess with me* vibes, and are also good if you have a tendency to panic in crowded places, at big parties, or in elevators.

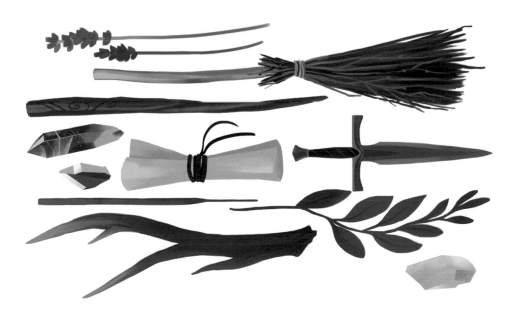

MAGICKAL SYMBOLS

CELTIC SYMBOLS

The AWEN or three suns for happiness and confidence

• popularity • getting noticed positively • for succeeding at interviews, auditions, or competitions •

The TRISKELE or magick spiral for calling who or what you most want in your life

• protecting yourself against bullies and those who are spiteful • travel • bringing together different parts of your life that are pulling you different ways • bringing peace to family or friends •

VIKING RUNE MAGICKAL SYMBOLS

THE HAMMER OF THOR, for protection against all harm and for a sudden burst of strength or stamina.

• guards against jealousy, cliques, physical attack, or danger • people who try to steal credit for your ideas or break up love or friendship through spite • threats and curses and bad spirits • for exciting dates and other activities •

TIWAZ, the guiding star, for good fortune and for aiming for success
• doing well in exams • winning scholarships, apprenticeships, internships, or the right college placement • overcoming fears, especially of flying • travel, especially overseas or interstate • standing out from the crowd (in the best way!) •

EGYPTIAN HIEROGLYPHS

The SCARAB for fierce protection if your confidence is being crushed
• protection against spite and online trolls • starting again after being let down by friends or someone special • preventing loss, theft, or damage of precious items • new opportunities after a disappointment •

ANKH for love, life, and new beginnings
• making new friends • starting over better than before if you have failed a major exam • increasing your magickal powers, charisma, and radiance

EYE OF HORUS, protection against envy and anyone who wishes you harm
• discovering the truth • protection against bad influences • a sudden brilliant solution to an old problem •

PLANETARY SIGNS

You have already learned about the zodiac birth signs and by now will have copied them into your Book of Shadows. As suggested previously, you can etch your personal sign for power and protection invisibly or physically on a candle for extra power and protection. You can also put these birth signs invisibly on jewelry or crystals or buy a birthstone pendant as listed on **PAGES 40–43**.

The planetary signs are even more powerful symbols of power and can be used regardless of your birth sign. However, I have listed the zodiac signs they rule so you can add your planet sign on the other side of the zodiac birth candle to give extra power when you are doing zodiac spells.

The Sun: rules Leo, July 23–August 23
• Achieving big dreams • getting noticed • popularity and leadership •

The Moon: rules Cancer, June 22–July 22
This is the magickal sign of the three phases of the moon
• secrets and secret love • protection against all harm • to balance hormones • knowing what people are thinking and feeling • keeping a low profile if you don't want to be noticed •

Mercury: rules Gemini, May 22–June 21 and Virgo, August 24–September 22
• To talk yourself into a high school or college placement, vacation, job, or internship • to give brilliant presentations • impressing people • to talk yourself out of trouble • to get away from emotional vampires • learning new things fast • for protection against liars and false friends •

Venus: rules Taurus, April 21–May 21 and Libra, September 23–October 23
• faithfulness in love • beauty and charisma • self-confidence • fighting inequality or violence against women •

Mars: rules Aries, March 21–April 20
• courage • independence • physical strength and fitness • to call the right love • to overcome prejudice • the power to ask for what you want • to face bullies •

Jupiter: rules Sagittarius, November 23–December 21
• putting things right • staying with a new habit • awards and scholarships • success in exams • money •

celebrations as well other special rites for all sorts of occasions, from birthdays to New Year's.

GETTING YOUR COVEN STARTED

You will need someone in your group who has a talent for organization to arrange the more mundane aspects of coven running. These will include buying candles, keeping track of the communal fund, deciding where and when to meet, and checking out a quiet outdoor spot for special seasonal rituals.

You can take turns leading rituals and activities. You may find different members have special skills like creating chants, writing ceremonies, or making seasonal decorations. Some people always like staying behind the scenes, maybe doing valuable tasks like updating the Book of Shadows. You can have one for the group as well as a private one. Your behind-the-scenes person can also make sure everyone has received an email containing the words you'll be using in the coming rituals. You may also have a natural poet in the group or someone who can play music—drums are great for raising the power.

At your first meeting, settle on how the coven is going to be run. Use this to set the next four or five dates so everyone knows where, when, and how you are going to meet. You can change the venue regularly if you want. However, if there is a spare garage or shed you can use regularly and decorate appropriately, that is ideal. You could even paint a circle with the quarters on the floor, covering it with a rug.

Build in a monthly planning meeting so you can talk over any problems with the way the coven is going. At this meeting you can brainstorm new ideas or maybe lead a dream-interpretation session or a past-life meditation to see when you were all witches together in another time.

Finally, you need a scribe for a collective Book of Shadows to record the chants you have learned or created and any special ceremonies you carry out.

If you meet someone else you'd like to invite to join, or word gets around that something pretty special is happening, make sure the whole group agrees on the newcomer. Magickal cliques are total disasters.

Magick grows quite naturally, and there is no right or wrong way to do magick, but you should always do it for good reasons and with love in your heart. As long as you do so, goodness and light will flow from your magickal workings.

CHOOSING THE COVEN NAME

Maybe after the first drawing down the moon or a quiet ritual together, brainstorm a name for your coven, or ask the moon goddess.

Pass around a crystal, and let her speak through each of you. Toss around ideas until one feels right to everyone. The name should ideally be just three or four words. Maybe name your coven after a favorite goddess, flower, crystal, nature spirit, angel, fairy-tale character, or magickal movie hero/ine. You could even use the name of a magickal animal, such as Pegasus, the winged horse, or the phoenix, who is reborn every five hundred years. Closer to home, choose a beautiful type of bird or animal that is found only in your home area.

The word *witch* is applied to both men and women. If you live in a unique location, you could be the Coven of the Snowy Mountains, or the Merfolk if your homes are close to the ocean. Are there any magickal legends of creatures that live in your area?

COVEN ACTIVITIES

You can plan day trips to local places of beauty. You may enjoy weekends camping or in a cabin near a beautiful lake. Here you can cast magick in a circle of trees, rocks, or a fairy mushroom circle. In folklore it is said you should run around the outside of a fairy mushroom circle nine times counterclockwise to avoid being enchanted. You can even draw your circle on the shore by the ocean and afterward let the tide carry it away.

Make or buy similar robes for everyone for special rituals. You may want cloaks for outdoor magick in cooler weather.

Shop together for major items. This is a good excuse for days at craft and antique fairs and garage sales.

SETTING UP YOUR COVEN ALTAR AND TOOLS

You can use your personal wands and athames in coven activities. But you should have a communal athame, wand, salt and water dish, central symbol dish, and bell for your coven altar.

You will need a table and altar cloths for your coven altar wherever you meet. If you are using someone's bedroom, they can clear their altar for the evening and replace everything with the chosen coven treasures.

You already have your personal magickal treasure box, but you will need a larger treasure box for your coven tools and materials.

Fill it with the same items as in your personal magickal box plus inks and a quill or nib pen for writing special messages at celebrations. Check the list of items on PAGES 10–12 to remind you. In practice, it is easier to have a collective set of everything rather than using your personal magickal supplies, so the coven can operate regardless of who comes.

You can keep your coven box in the house of the person with the most room, to be taken along to meetings. If you're lucky enough to have a permanent meeting place, then of course keep your coven altar already set and your treasure box there. If not, you can pack away the coven items in the box along with the supplies, ready for next time.

You will need a collective fund for your coven materials. Choose one person to check that the coven supplies are topped up and to keep track of the money.

DEDICATING YOURSELVES TO THE MAGICKAL CAUSE

Once you have your coven, you need to dedicate yourselves to the magickal craft and promise only to do magick for good or protective purposes, never in revenge or anger. Print the following dedication for each member to learn in advance, or create your own coven dedication.

1. As a group, go to a forest or wooded area where there is a natural circle of trees and stand in the center.

2. Each of you should choose a tree and stand with your back to it.

3. The first person turns around slowly nine times deosil, or clockwise, in front of the tree and says nine times,
   "I (say magick name aloud or silently) am a witch/wiseman/woman (or whatever name feels right for you), and I dedicate myself to the coven of (name), which I join willingly. I can leave whenever I choose without any other member acting or speaking against me. I will not share the magickal secrets I learn with my coven with anyone outside my coven."

4. Each person does the same in turn.

5. Now the first person turns slowly around nine times widdershins, or counterclockwise, in front of their

chosen tree, saying nine times slowly, *"I ask for wisdom and enlightenment from the wise ones, the ancestors and the angels. I promise to only work magick for the greatest good and with love and never in the spirit of anger or revenge, no matter how provoked. But I can and will defend myself and those I love from all harm magickally, without harming the person doing wrong."*

6. The others in turn again turn widdershins in front of their own trees, repeating the second set of words and actions.

7. Finally, the first person turns around slowly nine times clockwise once more and says slowly nine times again, *"I am a witch/wiseman/woman."* The others follow in turn.

8. Each person sits against the trunk of their chosen tree, closes their eyes, and allows its strength and wisdom to enter their minds as images, words, and sounds.

9. Mark your personal tree with a ribbon or write your initials, including your magick name, in the earth at the base of the tree with a stick, leave a crystal, and bury an offering. Return after a year and a day to renew your dedication.

10. Spend some time in the open air, finding special stones and natural objects to take home and adorn your coven altar.

CHAPTER 14

☀ COVEN RITUALS AND ☀ SEASONAL CELEBRATIONS

You have already moved on to more exciting ways of doing rituals, which are just longer spells. You have also learned to cast circles and welcome the guardians. Now you have everything you need to know to work with your coven to create beautiful rituals together.

Here are more ways you can jazz up rituals as a coven, including special rituals for Sabbats, the magickal holidays that occur throughout the year. These seasonal rituals are fun ways witches have celebrated for hundreds of years. You can fit your seasonal celebrations to coincide with modern festivals.

For example, the December winter celebration is perfect for Thanksgiving or Christmas, and the March spring festival is great for Easter. Samhain, at the end of October, is also Halloween, and you can add spooky masks and carve pumpkins as part of the ceremony, which can spill over into the spookiest party ever.

RAISING THE POWER

You are going to be moving and shaking once you and your coven get together magickally to raise power. In your own personal spells, you raised power by enchanting a symbol in a dish with your wand. But with a coven, you can have even more fun dancing in a circle.

Hold hands as you spin faster and faster, one turn going clockwise followed by one turn going counterclockwise, and so on. This gets the spell or ritual energies flying until you are ready to leap in the air or fall down as the spell flies free.

If you prefer, spiral in a conga-type line around the altar, with a drummer keeping time if possible. If no drummer, get someone to bang saucepan lids, or the coven can stamp, clap, and chant prearranged words, faster and louder. You might say, "Earth, Air, Water, Fire, bring to this (season/ritual) what we desire," faster and faster till everyone stamps, shouts the final word, and claps or jumps in the air. At this point the power of the spell or season is released as rainbow fireworks. For the seasonal celebrations, you could just chant the season name over and over faster and louder ("Welcome spring, grow everything"). The more repetitive and simple the chant is, the better to build the power and send it through the cosmos. You all then shout, "The power is free," as it all goes hurtling out into the universe. You can do clapping, stamping, and drumming on your own as well.

SEASONAL FESTIVALS

One difference between a simple spell and seasonal celebration is that you're going to need a much bigger dish in which to pile offerings from several people. See the suggestions in the list of the festivals on **PAGE 114** for good offerings depending on your wishes. Once you've cast the circle, everyone in turn puts their offering in the dish, which you are holding in front of the altar, facing outward. Each makes a wish as they put their offering in. Send out the list in advance to let your coven know what the festival is for and what suitable offerings to make are.

Magical Food and Drink

In seasonal rituals you are going to use a chalice filled with juice or wine. This time set it to the right of center of your altar. You will pass it around the circle and drink in turn from it after you've let the festival power free. And, of course, when you have something to drink, you want something to eat as well. Following the rules of old magick, you're going to have a dish of honey cakes or cookies to the left of the center of the altar.

Carrying out Coven Seasonal Ceremonies

* Your coven poet can write some suitable words for each part of the ceremony in advance and email everyone a copy to print out.

* Rehearse the chants and dances before the ceremony, maybe at a special meeting.

* In seasonal ceremonies, the form and order are slightly different for when you use the salt, incense, etc., to fill your symbol with power in a spell. It is the words and actions of the people doing the celebration that build up the power to launch the energies.

* Seasonal ceremonies are a good chance to dress up in the colors and flowers I have listed for each ceremony.

The Ceremony

1. Light any candles and incense on a central table or flat rock to serve as an altar. Cover it with a cloth that is the color of the festival (see **PAGES 114–120**).

2. Set the offerings bowl in the center of the altar.

3. Cast your circle around the altar and around anyone present who will be standing in the circle.

4. If you wish, greet the guardians of the four quarters or choose four people to do this.

5. The person leading the festival welcomes those present, saying something about the festival. The leader will make sure the different parts of the ceremony follow in the right order.

6. A second person, the spirit of the festival, would also stand in the center of the circle. S/he can be dressed imaginatively, for example with a sun headdress if standing for the rebirth of the sun at Midwinter.

7. Each person in turn is invited to place their offering in the offering bowl in front of the altar and make a wish or blessing. If all the offerings to be made won't fit, set the full offerings bowl in front of the altar on the ground after you've held it. Then pile extra offerings around it.

8. When all offerings are made, the person leading the ceremony lifts the offering dish while facing the altar. S/he asks for the blessings of the season and any special needs of those present.

9. When the dish is back in the center, you all circle-dance and chant. This raises the energy of the season so the power shoots into the air and flows back as good things/ protection of the season or whatever you asked for.

10. The leader/spirit of the season says, "The power is free."

The Cakes and Chalice Part of the Ceremony

1. Everyone returns to their place in the circle and stands silently, letting the energies settle.
2. The leader takes the cakes and, holding them high while facing the altar, asks that they may be blessed by the power of the season (name the season).
3. The spirit of the season touches the cakes with the ritual knife as the above blessing is spoken.
4. Now the spirit of the season lifts the chalice while the leader puts the wand into the liquid and asks that the chalice be blessed by the powers of the season. In old magick these actions stand for the joining of the God and Goddess in love.
5. The leader asks, after cakes and chalice have been blessed, that there will be peace and harmony in the world and enough for everyone to eat.
6. Moving clockwise, the leader takes the cakes around the circle, gives everyone one, and says, "Blessings."
7. The person receiving the cake replies, "Blessings," and eats it.
8. The spirit of the season follows around the circle and offers the chalice to each person. Everyone in turn sips the juice. If anyone doesn't want to drink from a shared cup, they can just say, "Blessings," and not drink.
9. The plate and chalice are returned to the altar.
10. The guardians, if called at the beginning, are thanked by the leader or the four chosen people. The parting words, "Until we meet again," are spoken by him/her at each quarter.
11. The celebration ends with the leader asking a blessing for the world and that everyone's personal seasonal wishes be

granted, and everyone replies as one, "Blessings be on all."

12. The circle is uncast and all candles blown out.
13. The incense is left to burn.
14. Celebrate!
15. Any offerings can be scattered afterward on the ground away from the circle in honor of the earth mother. However, if there are flowers, fruits, or vegetables, you might like to donate them where they will be appreciated or needed.

SEASONAL CELEBRATIONS

The equinox and solstice dates may vary slightly each year depending on the cycle of leap years. Check online to confirm dates.

IMBOLC: THE FESTIVAL OF LIGHT
January 31–February 2

• New ideas • first love • first steps to new love or trust • plan a new project • for overcoming depression or anxiety • looking forward to the future • helping younger people •

THE RITUAL: Light candles all around your room to return light to the world and hope for a brilliant year ahead for you.

OFFERINGS: Milk, honey, candles, seeds, early budding flowers, and greenery

INCENSES, FLOWERS, AND HERBS: Angelica, basil, crocus, heather, myrrh, snowdrops, and violets

CANDLE COLORS: Pale pink, green, blue, and white

FESTIVAL FOODS: Seed bread, milk, honey, any seeds, hot milky drinks, cheese, and butter

OSTARA OR THE SPRING EQUINOX: THE FESTIVAL OF EGGS AND FERTILITY
March 20–March 22

• Making changes in your life • friends and activities • growing love • new beginnings and chances • travel • house moves • spring-cleaning your room and life •

THE RITUAL: Paint and decorate the shells of boiled eggs and set them in a basket of flowers and greenery. Dedicate each to a new beginning you desire. Float the basket on water.

OFFERINGS: Eggs (especially painted or chocolate ones), feathers, spring flowers or leaves, a sprouting pot of seeds, pottery rabbits and birds, and feathers

INCENSES, FLOWERS, AND HERBS: Daffodil, honeysuckle, hyacinth, lemon, primroses, sage, and thyme

CANDLE COLORS: Yellow and green

FESTIVAL FOODS: Decorated boiled eggs, chocolate rabbits, hot cross buns, and lamb

BELTAINE: LINKED WITH MAY DAY, THE FESTIVAL OF FLOWERS
April 30–May 2

• Doing well in study • training and money-spinning ideas • going steady • special love • improving health and fitness • a big push forward if things have been stuck • looking beautiful and radiant •

THE RITUAL: Light twin red candles and sprinkle salt in each flame saying, I take the power of fertility/creativity into myself, asking that (make wish). Blow out your candles, relight, repeat the wish and leave the candles to burn.

OFFERINGS: Fresh greenery, flowers and blossoms, and ribbons

INCENSES, FLOWERS, AND HERBS: Almond, angelica, bluebells, frankincense, lilac, marigolds, rosemary, and roses; also, any flower or light floral fragrance

CANDLE COLORS: Dark green, scarlet, and silver

FESTIVAL FOODS: Any roasted meat, traditional oatmeal cake cut into thirteen portions (or one piece for each person present; the person drawing a piece marked beforehand with a cross traditionally has to pay a forfeit or entertain those present with a song), egg custard dishes, any miniature delicacies said to be left by the fairies whose festival it is, elderflower, and berry jams

MIDSUMMER, LITHA, OR SUMMER SOLSTICE, FESTIVAL OF SUNLIGHT AND GOLD
June 20–June 22

• Feeling powerful • happiness • success in every way • adventures • offers for future career paths • seizing chances • success in tests, exams, or interviews • strength and fitness • self-confidence • loving yourself as you are • going for leadership • seizing chances when you have to act fast •

THE RITUAL: Weave seven different kinds or colors of flowers on to a copper circlet on Solstice morn at dawn. Hang it on a tree and dance seven times clockwise round the tree, calling love, happiness, health or whatever you most desire. At sunset hang the circlet on your bedroom wall and leave it there until the flowers fade.

OFFERINGS: Brightly colored flowers, oak boughs, golden fern pollen that is said to reveal buried treasure wherever it falls, ribbons (in gold, scarlet, orange, and yellow), gold-colored coins, gold jewelry, any golden fruit or vegetable

INCENSES, FLOWERS, AND HERBS: Chamomile, fennel, frankincense, lavender,   marigolds, orange, rosemary, sage, and any flowers (gold, red, or orange)

CANDLE COLORS: Red, orange, and gold

FESTIVAL FOODS: Red and yellow fruits and vegetables • spices • honey • ham • butter and cheese • orange juice •

LAMMAS OR LUGHNASADH, FESTIVAL OF THE FIRST HARVEST
July 31–August 2

• Justice • dealing with authority • saving money • serious love • journeys to see family, friends, or love far away • keeping promises • giving up bad habits and people who are bad for you •

THE RITUAL: Weave dried grasses into knots and tie with red ribbon. Burn your grasses/grain in a deep fire bucket and when cool scatter the ashes around a plant you have dedicated to the regrowth of a desire or dream.

OFFERINGS: Any straw object (such as a corn doll, a corn knot, or a straw hat tied with red ribbon), poppies or cornflowers, a small container of mixed cereals, dried grasses, stones with natural holes, and freshly baked bread

INCENSES, FLOWERS, AND HERBS: Cinnamon, ginger, heather, sunflowers, and any dark yellow, deep blue, or brown-gold flowers

CANDLE COLORS: Golden brown or dark yellow

FESTIVAL FOODS: Homemade bread, milk, cereal products, elderberry and fruit juices, strawberries, berry pies and fruit juices, potato soup, popcorn, sweet corn, and chicken

MABON, OR AUTUMN EQUINOX, FESTIVAL OF THE SECOND HARVEST
September 21–September 23

• Finishing tasks • mending quarrels • forgiving yourself for mistakes • the return of money owed • getting rid of what didn't work out • sticking with loyal people and long-term goals • sick relatives getting better •

THE RITUAL: Fill a basket with autumn/Fall leaves and another with nuts or berries. Cast a leaf on to the ground naming what you wish to shed or leave behind. Then eat a nut or berry naming what you want to take forward to the months ahead. Continue until all are gone or you have fulfilled your wishes.

OFFERINGS: Leaves (copper-colored, yellow, or orange), willow boughs, harvest fruits (apples, berries, and nuts), copper or bronze coins, copper jewelry, and model geese or ducks.

INCENSES, FLOWERS, AND HERBS: Ferns, geranium, Michaelmas daisies, myrrh, pine, sandalwood, and all small-petal purple and blue flowers

CANDLE COLORS: Blue or green

FESTIVAL FOODS: Fruit, vegetables, jam, nuts, apple pies, venison or chicken, and potatoes

HALLOWEEN, SAMHAIN (SOW-win), FESTIVAL OF THE BEGINNING OF WINTER
October 31–November 2

• Protection, both psychic and physical • remembering relatives who have passed away • overcoming fears, especially of ghosts and bad spirits • saying goodbye to people who are holding us back •

THE RITUAL: Light a single purple candle facing the West and surround it with small garlic cloves. Ask your ancestors to come and offer you their wisdom. Pick up a pen and allow your ancestors to guide your hand with messages. Afterwards extinguish the candle.

OFFERINGS: Apples, carved pumpkins and lanterns (light them and place them around the outside of the circle), nuts, autumn leaves, and salt

INCENSES, FLOWERS, AND HERBS: Ferns, garlic, large white flowers, nutmeg, pine, rose petals/fragrances, sage, thyme, and any spices

CANDLE COLOR: Orange and purple

FESTIVAL FOODS: Roasted beef, salted fish and pickles, pumpkin pie and soup, baked and toffee apples with spices, baked potatoes, spiced or mulled cider, and candies and sweets of all kinds

YULE, OR MIDWINTER SOLSTICE, THE RETURN OF THE SUN

December 20–22

• Happiness at home and family harmony • reconnect with old friends • planning get-togethers, parties, and fun • spending time with older relatives • patience with family and close friends • planning and receiving surprises •

THE RITUAL: Light a circle of white candles with a smaller central white candle in the center. Extinguish all but the central candle and say, Wise grandmother of Winter, I will walk into the darkness with you, trusting you will restore to me the light. Sit by the light of the single candle and then relight the outer circle of candles one by one.

SYMBOLS: Evergreen boughs (especially pine or fir), small logs of wood (especially oak, pine, and ash), holly and ivy, silver and gold ribbons and baubles, silver jewelry, and small wrapped gifts for everyone present (given after the ceremony)

INCENSES, FLOWERS, AND HERBS: Bay, cedar, frankincense and myrrh, holly, juniper, pine, poinsettias, rosemary, sage and all spices, and scarlet and white flowers

CANDLE COLORS: White, scarlet, gold, and purple

FESTIVAL FOODS: Turkey, thick meat and vegetable stews, cakes with marzipan and icing, rich fruit cake and puddings (traditionally with silver and gold charms or coins hidden inside), and mince pies

✳ AFTERWORD ✳

Though this book is chock-full of information, and you will learn a great deal more as you continue to study the Craft, always remember, that true magick comes from your heart.

You don't need to learn a thousand different rules; let the words and the actions come from within. Let those old, kind witch guardians of centuries past talk to you in your dreams and as you cast your spells.

Remember, you are of immense value as you are and who you are now. Don't let anyone bully you, criticize you, or make you feel bad or useless.

Use your magick wisely and *always* for good. In that way you will find that you draw to you all those good things you want, need, and deserve, and drive away the fears and the negative people through your own magickal light. Remember, light is stronger than darkness, and blessings are stronger than curses.

May you always walk in the light of the love of others and, most importantly, your own fabulous radiance. If you believe in yourself, that light can never be put out. It is said that all the darkness in the world cannot put out a single candle lit in love and hope. May the Goddess hold you lovingly in the palm of her hand until we meet again.

Cassandra Eason, March 2019

READY-MADE SPELLS

Now that you've learned the basics, here are some ready-made spells for when you are in a hurry and don't have time to make up your own. They cover many wishes and needs.

You can also use these spells as templates for creating your own spells. You will notice that they don't all follow every stage of spellcasting separately. As you become more experienced, you will find you can join stages together.

CONFIDENCE AND POPULARITY

MAKE NEW FRIENDS

You will need

* A photo of you hiding your face on the screen of your computer, tablet, or smartphone

* A second photo on a second screen of you smiling

* Yellow ribbons

Timing

If you've got a social event you're dreading

The spell

1. Look at the picture of you on the screen hiding your face and say, *"I am shy, don't know why. World, I know you would like me, if only I can show what fun I can be."*

2. Delete the hiding selfie image.

3. Frame the picture of yourself smiling on the second screen with a bright border, saying, *"Little Ms./Mr. Shyness has gone away, the confident new Ms./Mr. is here to stay."*

4. Print out the smiling picture and hang it in your room, surrounded by yellow ribbons.

BOOST YOUR CONFIDENCE

You will need

 ✳   A mirror

 ✳   A soft white cloth

Timing

   When sunlight shines in the mirror

The spell

1. Gaze into the mirror, saying, *"I look and see, what you say about me, fat, stupid, ugly. Wait a minute, no, what I see, reflected in me is only your malice and jealousy."*

2. Polish the mirror in counterclockwise circles, saying, *"Beautiful/gorgeous, smart I am and beautiful/gorgeous smart shall I be, once I step right away, from your twisted image of me."*

3. Move away from the mirror with one last smile and go into the sunshine.

FACING CHANGE

You will need

- ❋   A green plant in a pot to keep on your altar, with lots of small branches or stems

- ❋   Seven orange ribbons for confidence

- ❋   Seven small bells (you can buy the bells in a packet at any gift or bargain store)

Timing

Seven days before the new event

The spell

1. Tie the first bell to the plant with the ribbon and ring the bell, saying, *"I ring the bell, my fears do go, all will be fine, that I know."*

2. Each day add another bell and ribbon, saying the same words. Ring the new bell, and, afterward, ring each bell fastened to the plant.

3. If you worry at any time during the week, ring all the bells that are on the plant and say, *"I am strong, I am brave, the future's fine, I make it mine."*

4. On the eighth day, take the plant and bells with you if you are moving to a new home. Before you start a new school or head out to meet new people, ring the bells fast one after the other, saying again, *"I am strong, I am brave, the future's fine, I make it mine."*

COMBAT STRESS

You will need

* ✳ Your favorite tea. Chamomile is especially soothing

* ✳ A mug of boiling water

* ✳ A teaspoon

Timing

When needed

The spell

1. When you start to panic or are being hassled to do something fast or someone is pressurizing you for a decision or answer, stop. Make a mug of tea or coffee.

2. Make an excuse to go away from the crowd for a minute or two, and switch your smartphone to silent mode.

3. Stir the cup nine times counterclockwise, saying, *"Calm and peace, this stress must cease. You (name worst culprit/s or stressful event) scramble my brain, yet quiet and calm shall I remain."*

4. Stir nine times counterclockwise again, saying the same words nine more times.

5. Stop and, when you are ready, slowly sip your drink. When you have had enough, pour the rest away under a running tap, saying, *"Pressure and hassle flow away, calm I shall remain this day."*

A WANING MOON SPELL FOR TAKING AWAY FEAR

You will need

* A bowl of water in a glass or silver-colored bowl

Timing

The waning moon, two or three days after the full moon, outdoors

The spell

1. Hold the bowl up to the moon or to the sky if you can't see the moon. Then place the bowl on the ground. Wash your hands in the water, saying, "I wash my hands in Grandmother Moon, asking she will take away my fear/worry (name) soon."

2. Scatter water drops on the center of your brow, your throat, and your inner wrist points, repeating the words.

3. Tip the rest of the water onto the ground.

FULFILLING WISHES AND DREAMS

BRING ON VACATION!

You will need

* Three balloons (yellow for exciting short adventures, summer school, or sports or arts training camps; use blue for overseas travel, backpacking, or interstate travel; also use blue if you want to move away to college)

Timing

Three days in an open space

The spell

1. On the first day, take the first balloon to the open space. Holding the balloon, name the place and time you wish to travel and with whom.

2. Let the balloon tug in your hand as you lift it upward to catch the breeze. Say nine times, *"Carry my wish high into the sky, that to (name place and time) I will fly."*

3. Let the balloon go, calling, *"The wish is free, and so shall come to me, my dreamed-of travel opportunity (name what you want again and the time)."*

4. Turn around and do not watch the balloon.

5. Repeat the wish on the next two days with new balloons.

GOOD LUCK

A DICE SPELL FOR GOOD LUCK

You will need

* Six dice
* A picture of yourself looking happy
* A small purse or drawstring bag
* A jar of dried supermarket mint

Timing

Wednesday and Friday are lucky days

The spell

1. Toss the dice in your closed hands higher and faster, saying, *"Roll the dice, shake the dice, twice the luck, twice as nice. Everything will turn out right (name anything special you need luck for)."*

2. Allow the dice to scatter on the photo. The numbers do not matter, but six is especially lucky.

3. Pick up the dice and repeat the shaking, chanting, and throwing six times.

4. Transfer the dice to the bag. Add six pinches of dried mint and close the bag. Toss the bag six times over the photo, higher and higher as you chant faster.

5. On the sixth throw, catch the bag and end the chant with a shout. *"Luck, lucky, luckier will I be, I am so close to victory, winner takes all, I cannot fail. I will not fall."*

6. Keep the bag of dice and mint on top of the photo on your altar and carry it any time you need extra good luck.

TURN BAD LUCK INTO GOOD

You will need

* ✳ A purple candle placed to the left of the central white altar candle
* ✳ A candlesnuffer or old teaspoon

Timing

Thursday, day of Barakiel, Archangel of Good Fortune

The spell

1. Invisibly trace with your index finger on the unlit purple candle, *Bad luck begone.*

2. Trace invisibly on the unlit white candle, *Good luck fast come.*

3. Light the purple candle, saying, *"Bad luck enter here no more, I shut the door."*

4. Light the white candle from the purple one, saying, *"Good luck welcome, in you come."*

5. Extinguish the purple candle with the snuffer, saying, *"Bad luck, dark luck, begone, your power is done."*

6. Leave the white candle to burn, saying, *"Lucky and luckier shall I be, great good fortune shall I see."*

LOVE

ATTRACT NEW LOVE

You will need

* A map or drawn plan you make showing your school and neighborhood

* A wider map of the city/state in which you live or, if you internet date, the whole of your country

* A box of pins

* A magnet

* A pincushion or padded cloth to hold the pins in the spell

Timing

Any night from crescent moon until full moon

The spell

1. Scatter the pins over the map, saying, *"Near and far o'er land and sea, a love that is true, I call to me. That when the time is right we shall meet, whether from far away or in the next street. As pin to magnet, flower to honeybee, I ask true love to come to me."*

2. Circle the magnet clockwise over the whole map, collecting the pins one by one and putting them at the side of the map.

3. When you have a whole pin pile next to the map, stick each in the pincushion, saying the same words slowly until you have finished.

4. Fold the map with the magnet inside in a drawer and place your pincushion in the center of your altar.

5. Go somewhere new, join a new school club, or go with your friends to a place where you might meet new people in the weeks after the spell.

LET'S DANCE!

You will need

- ✳ A mirror

- ✳ Six tealights or small white candles along the edge of the mirror

Timing

After dark

The spell

1. Put on your prettiest dress or favorite outfit. Carefully, so you don't burn yourself or your clothes, light the candles left to right. Look in the mirror, saying, *"All dressed up, nowhere to go, a gorgeous girl/guy like me you know, can't hesitate, just won't wait. So please ask me to be your date (name anyone you would like to ask you or you'd like to ask if you weren't too shy)."*

2. Leave the candles to burn.

3. If you haven't been asked in a couple of days, issue the invite yourself, using the confidence and charisma you've got from the spell.

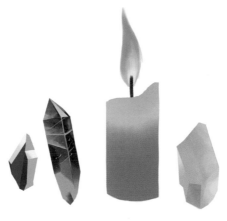

TO DETER BULLIES

Remember, it's the nastiness toward you that you're banishing, not the people.

You will need

* ❋ Pictures from social media of the ringleaders, or their names typed in a row

Timing

Wednesday, the day that protects you from spite

The spell

1. Point to the first picture on the left of the screen with your index finger of your writing hand, saying, *"Bully girl/boy, smirking in a row, ganging up together, off you go."*

2. Delete the picture from the screen.

3. Continue the spell until only one face is left on the screen. Say, *"One bully boy/girl, left all alone, your power over me is done, I have won."*

4. Delete the image, substituting a happy picture of yourself with good friends.

PROTECTION FROM UNFRIENDLY GHOSTS

Rose water is very good for protection against anything paranormal. You can buy this from a pharmacy or use a rose cologne, However, it is extra special to make your own.

> ✳ **TIP:** Add a tablespoon of rose petals to a cup of hot but not boiling water, leave for fifteen minutes, and then strain. Remove the rose petals and shake the mixture.

You will need

- ✳ A small bowl to hold the rose water
- ✳ A rose-scented candle
- ✳ Your ritual knife

Timing

Just before it gets dark

The spell

1. Light the candle in the center of your bedroom and pass your hands over the rose water. Move your writing hand clockwise and the other counterclockwise, palms flat and facing down. As you do so, say three times, *"May only goodness and light remain in this place."*

2. Make a cross on the surface of the rose water with your athame and say, *"May only goodness and light remain in this place."*

3. Dip the index and middle finger of your writing hand into the rose water bowl or use a small leafy twig.

4. Sprinkle a few drops of rose water on the inside and outside of the door handles of your room and the window catches all around your bedroom.

5. Sprinkle it also around the outside of your altar table and the corners of the head and foot of your bed while saying, *"May only goodness and light remain in this place."*

6. Leave the bowl of water in the center of your altar and top it up regularly.

GOSSIP BEGONE!

You will need

∗ A crystal pendant with any blue crystal

∗ A frankincense or sandalwood incense stick in a holder to the right of the pendant

Timing

Saturday, day of Saturn and protection

The spell

1. Light the incense. Over and around the pendant, draw clockwise with incense stick smoke in the air the shape of the Eye of Horus (see **PAGE** 97). Hold the unlit end and use the lighted end of the incense stick like a smoke pen.

2. If you prefer, draw an ordinary eye shape in smoke.

3. Say as you do so, *"Turn away the eye of envy and jealousy from me, think not of me (name the jealous person or people), speak not of me*

enviously. Look not at me spitefully, so shall it be. I wish you no harm, I send you peace, but this envy now must cease."

4. Leave the incense to burn.

5. As you wear the crystal, the invisible eye will protect you.

STUDY AND TRAINING

IMPROVE MEMORY AND CONCENTRATION

You will need

* ∗ A natural creamy yellow beeswax candle

* ∗ Parchment paper or a small nonstick tray

* ∗ A mixture of sage, rosemary, and thyme dried kitchen herbs, all good for memory and revising or learning new things

Timing

A week before any test, presentation, or exam

The spell

1. Scatter the herbs on the paper.

2. Warm the candle very gently with a hair dryer (do not light yet). Roll it in the plate of dried herbs, saying, *"Sage, rosemary, and thyme, let good memory be mine."*

3. Before lighting, stand the candle in a heatproof bowl of sand or soil, as a candle rolled in herbs can spit a bit toward the end of burning.

4. Light it, saying, *"As this wax flows, so my memory blocks go, I will recall what I need, success shall be mine indeed."*

5. Let the candle burn, and bury any remaining wax beneath a growing plant or tree, saying, *"Easy will learning be, knowledge flows into me."*

PASS WITH FLYING COLORS

You will need

*   A mirror in which you can see your head and shoulders

*   A blue bag or purse in front of the mirror

*   On top of the purse or bag, place a blue and gold lapis lazuli, a green aventurine, your own birth crystal or gem, a citrine, and a clear quartz. If you can't get these, use a blue, green, yellow, clear, or white crystal, and one the same color as your birthstone (see **PAGES 40–43** for the list)

Timing

The morning of the exam, audition, interview, or competition

The spell

1. Place the crystals in the bag or purse and close it.

2. Facing the mirror, toss the bag five times, higher and higher, saying, *"Mirror, mirror on the wall, I shall not fail, I shall not fall, I shall succeed in every way, Mirror send success today."*

3. Throw the bag a sixth time and say as you catch it, *"Success is mine, mirror, like you, shall I shine."*

4. Take the crystal bag with you to the event.

A CUPCAKE PARTY WISH SPELL

You will need

* Ingredients or a mix to make cupcakes, cookies, or a large cake

* A sharp knife

* A mixing bowl and a mixing spoon

Timing

Friday evening

The spell:

1. Add the ingredients, then each of you in turn stirs the mix seven times clockwise, saying, *"May I be/have (make a wish) and be happy, healthy, in love and always lucky. May this happiness last, seven by seven years more, good fortune open for me the door."*

2. Then each person in the same order draws on the surface of the uncooked mix with the knife a word or symbol of love or happiness. This will be absorbed into the mix.

3. If making cupcakes or cookies, make one for each person present.

4. When cooked and cool, each person invisibly draws or writes the same symbol or word with the tip of a knife on their chosen cupcake or cookie.

5. Each says after marking the cake, *"Seven by seven years shall we be friends, the love between us shall never end."*

6. The same is done when the cake is iced, each writing in the icing with a knife visibly the word or symbol, and each saying again, *"Seven by seven years, shall we be friends, the love between us shall never end."*

7. If making a large cake, each person writes their symbol on it after baking. The cake is then cut into the number of slices as people present.

8. Eat the friendship cake/s.

DREAM OF A FUTURE LOVE

You will need

* Seven different kinds or colors of flowers, sufficient for everyone to decorate a circlet of flowers (if you can't get the seven, you can use white flowers instead of any other color and kind. Get everyone to bring some flowers)

* A small bendable wire circlet (copper for love) or a circlet made from vines or raffia for each of you (you can buy these ready-made circlets in craft stores or garden centers, or you can each make your own)

* Strong thread to tie the flowers on to the circlet

* A large bowl of water

Timing

Any evening just before sunset or Midsummer Eve as part of a Midsummer party or coven Solstice celebration

The Spell

1. Each of you ties the flowers with thread all around your own circlet, cutting the stems so they bend around the wire.

2. Afterward, chant together, *"With seven flowers sweet do I call thee, love. Come dance with me in my dreams and through the night till morning light."*

3. After making the flower circlets you can all go outdoors and dance around a tree or dance indoors, chanting the same words as you dance.

4. Make love wishes by each dropping a handful of petals from the spare flowers into a huge bowl of water.

5. To answer one another's questions, each says in turn as they drop the petals into the water, *"Flower angels or fairies show to me, what I most need to see."*

6. If you all look you will see pictures forming on the water's surface made by the shape of the floating petals (swirl the water to change the pictures). You can take it in turn to ask questions. Everyone can give messages that come into your heads about the pictures. Sunlight, bright moonlight, or gold candlelight will give you light pools on the water.

7. When you are finished, each of you should take home your circlet of flowers and hang it over your bed.

8. Before sleep say softly seven times, *"With seven flowers sweet do I call thee, love. Come dance with me in my dreams and through the night till morning light."*

9. Be sure to contact one another the next day to tell one another about your dreams.

REFERENCE

THE DAYS OF THE WEEK

Of course you can do magick anytime, any place. However, each day of the week is especially good for certain kinds of spells.

SUNDAY for Big Ambitions and Success

• confidence • new beginnings • happiness after difficulties • fathers and grandfathers • health and fitness • money • creative ventures • overcoming bad luck • standing out from the crowd •

Planet: Sun
Archangel: Michael
Color: Gold
Element: Fire
Crystals: Amber • carnelian • diamond • clear crystal quartz • tiger's eye • golden topaz
Incenses: Cloves • cinnamon • frankincense
Trees: Bay • birch • laurel
Herbs and oils: Chamomile • juniper • rosemary • saffron • St. John's wort
Metal: Gold

MONDAY for Happiness at Home and Family

• first love • renewal of love and trust • women, especially mothers and grandmothers • children and animals • secrets • psychic gifts •

Planet: Moon
Archangel: Gabriel
Color: Silver or translucent white
Element: Water
Crystals: Moonstone • mother-of-pearl • pearl • selenite • opal
Incense: Jasmine • myrrh • mimosa • lemon
Trees: Willow • alder
Herbs and oils: Lotus • poppy • wintergreen
Metal: Silver

TUESDAY for Courage and Independence

• overcoming seemingly impossible odds • resisting bullies • physical strength for anything you have to do • doing things your own way • succeeding in anything competitive, especially sports • standing up for what is right even if it makes you unpopular •

Planet: Mars
Archangel: Samael or Camael
Color: Red
Element: Fire
Crystals: Garnet • bloodstone • ruby • red jasper
Incense: Dragon's blood • all spices • ginger • mint • thyme
Trees: Cypress • holly • pine
Herbs and oils: Basil • cinnamon • coriander • garlic • pepper • tarragon
Metal: Iron • steel

WEDNESDAY for Learning New Things and All Study

• moneymaking • passing examinations and tests • short-distance travel and vacations for a few days • house or educational moves within the same town or state • protection against jealousy, spite, lies, online nastiness •

Planet: Mercury

Archangel: Raphael

Color: Yellow

Element: Air

Crystals: Yellow agate • citrine • falcon's eye • yellow jasper • malachite • onyx

Incense: Lavender • lemongrass • mace • nutmeg

Trees: Hazel • ash

Herbs and oils: Dill • fennel • parsley • valerian

Metal: Quicksilver (Mercury)

THURSDAY for Planning Your Future Career and Leadership

• long-distance travel • interstate house or education moves • going steady • loyal friends • making official complaints about unfairness • not taking matters in your own hands • working together with others on projects • getting rid of bad habits and bad influences on you •

Planet: Jupiter

Archangel: Sachiel

Color: Blue • purple

Element: Air

Crystals: Azurite • lapis lazuli • sodalite • turquoise

Incense: Agrimony • cedar • sandalwood • sage

Trees: Beech • oak (also ash)

Herbs and oils: Borage • cinquefoil • coltsfoot • hyssop • mistletoe

Metal: Tin

FRIDAY for Love and for Mending Quarrels

• loving yourself as you are • seeing your own beauty/attractiveness and radiating it • popularity • friendship • the growth of happiness and success in your life • reducing the influence of destructive people and those who never listen to what you want •

Planet: Venus

Archangel: Anael

Color: Green • pink

Element: Earth

Crystals: Amethyst • emerald • jade • moss agate • rose quartz

Incense: Geranium • rose • strawberry • vervain

Trees: Almond • apple • birch

Herbs and oils: Feverfew • mugwort • pennyroyal • verbena • yarrow

Metal: Copper

SATURDAY for Building Up Step-By-Step and Protection

• finding lost objects and missing pets • overcoming fears and phobias • anxiety and depression • feeling safe again if life is difficult • saving instead of spending for big items • saying no when people take advantage of you •

Planet: Saturn

Archangel: Cassiel

Colors: Brown • black • gray

Element: Earth

Crystals: Hematite • jet • lodestone • obsidian • smoky quartz

Incense: Mimosa • cypress • patchouli

Trees: Blackthorn • yew

Herbs: Aspen • bistort • comfrey • horsetail • Solomon's seal

Metal: Lead • pewter

MONTHS OF THE YEAR

Each month has its own powers, and favors particular kinds of spells. You can increase the power of a spell by also using the day of the week that shares similar powers.

JANUARY for New Beginnings and to Leave Behind Bad Habits and Fears

• To bring together different parts of your life • to combine work and study with developing a talent • stopping being pulled when two people demand you choose • mending quarrels •

FEBRUARY for New Love and for Increasing Good Luck

• melting coldness or indifference • planting the seeds of future success • for any cleansing/purification spells • for driving away what is destructive or redundant •

MARCH for Courage and Making Changes in Your Life

• action • activities • new sporting interests and fitness programs • solving old problems • new projects and ways of doing things • not following the crowd •

APRIL for Increasing Love and Believing in Yourself

• creative talents and projects • health and healing • successful study • making money through your talents • making new friends • being or becoming happy •

MAY for Travel and Travel Plans, Home and Family

• giving your room a makeover • getting unexpected help with your money • romance, maybe with someone you've known for ages as a friend • solving problems with family • getting on well with brothers and sisters •

JUNE for Joint Projects, Ventures, and Group Activities

• fun, parties, and celebrations with family and friends • doing really well at school, training, or work • joining new clubs and shared-interest groups on- and offline •

JULY for Leadership and Getting Recognized for Your Talents

• steps towards achieving long-term ambitions and dreams • successful auditions • winning prizes • overcoming any shyness or holding back from people or life •

AUGUST for Opening Doors

• succeeding where you failed • reversing bad luck • rewards for earlier plans and projects you'd given up on • finding or recovering what is lost •

SEPTEMBER for Putting Unfairness Right and Increasing Psychic Powers

• uncovering secrets • success in training, retraining, and tests • answering difficult questions • succeeding in projects and study where learning is hard • sharing your knowledge and getting credit for it •

OCTOBER for Success and Unexpectedly Good Invitations

• rewards and prizes where you've worked hard • learning new skills and technology • taking a chance and it paying off • going for what you really want now and in the long term •

NOVEMBER for Dreams Coming True and for Perfecting a Skill or Talent

• overcoming fears and those who make you feel bad • success in anything to do with authority and the law that has worried you • balancing the different people and parts of your life that seem to pull different ways •

DECEMBER for Completing Unfinished Ideas and Projects

• giving and receiving presents and rewards • finishing and sending off or submitting both overdue projects and creative ventures • enjoying quiet times with existing friends and family • planning for the future •

MAGICK NUMBER MEANINGS

ONE for New Beginnings and Standing Out from the Crowd

• energy • enthusiasm • doing it your own way • brainstorming and all creative ventures, talents, and projects • finding an original solution to an old problem • getting things moving after being stuck • fame and fortune •

TWO for Getting Along with People and For All Joint Projects

• putting together two different parts of your life • choosing between two people • feeling happy with yourself as you are • doubling anything such as success or money •

THREE for Gradual Growth in Everything

• anything that will take three months or three years to complete • welcoming new people into your family or life • joining a new group of friends • parties and fun events • going outside your comfort zone •

FOUR for Feeling Secure in Your Life and Achieving Solid Results That Will Secure Your Future

• accepting necessary rules and limits to get what you want in the long term • settled times at home or in your education/training • saving, not spending • solving money problems • choosing loyal friends over exciting but unreliable new ones •

FIVE for Travel and Success in Study and Learning Fast

• risks paying off • making quick decisions that are right • new methods and ways of doing things • successful online encounters and avoiding trolls or frauds • overcoming jealousy • talking your way to success and out of tight corners • interviews and anything media-based •

SIX for Love and for Happy Relationships With Family and Friends

• mending quarrels • peace and harmony at home • dealing with drama kings and queens without losing your cool • the gradual growth of self-confidence • not being pressured into being or doing what others want • adventures outdoors •

SEVEN for Amazing Good Luck and Psychic Powers

• impressing people even if you're not sure of your facts • romance • magical dreams • peaceful sleep • keeping and discovering secrets • moon magick • protection against those who would deceive you •

EIGHT for Power and Achievement

• for brilliant and original ideas that work out • for turning your life around if things just aren't working for you • all written assignments or projects and communication, on- and offline • standing up against people who are always right • sorting tangled money matters •

NINE for Acting, Not Waiting, and Not Accepting Second Best

• wanting the best in any and every part of your life and putting in the effort to get it • competitiveness, especially in sports • adventure vacations and activities • courage • stamina and physical fitness • fighting for justice for anyone who is in trouble or being treated unfairly • a noble warrior number •

TEN for Successfully Completing Any Goal and Looking Ahead to the Next Stages

• long-term achievements • being happy in yourself and your life • removing anyone or anything in your life that is holding you back • a major travel plan • joining an organization, creative academy, or sports training that will take you to the top but also away from home for a time •

USEFUL WEBSITES

Moon Phases Lunar Calendar, updated every year, gives moon times and phases for anywhere in the world. www.timeanddate.com/moon/phases

Moon Tracks Astrology Calendar tells you which zodiac sign the moon is in at any time in all its phases. www.moontracks.com/lunar_ingress.html

Farmers' Almanac gives dates, times, and names of full moons and the Native North American folklore around them. www.farmersalmanac.com/full-moon-dates-and-times

Solstices and Equinoxes seasonal calculator of solstices and equinoxes worldwide for the next ten years. www.timeanddate.com/calendar/seasons.html

INDEX